Wealthology

Creating Lasting Prosperity in an Uncertain World

By Akinaw Bulcha

Dedicated to anyone who......

... is smart enough to get that there's hidden gold in personal, business, and economic failures.

...is bold enough to have a dream.

...believes in themselves.

...is willing to question their assumptions.

...wants a solid foundation for making financial decisions.

...wants total control over their financial life.

...is looking for an easy, fun and motivational way to understand economics.

...doesn't have time to read lots of books.

...can see that "Wealthology" can only be learned after false assumptions have proven their worth.

...who wants to learn something once and move on with their life.

Table of Contents

Read This First!

It's not every day an author forbids readers from doing something with his book, but I'm doing just that for important reasons. You're forbidden from doing any of the following things:

1. You're forbidden from reading the last section of this book before reading the other sections first.

2. More importantly, you're forbidden from writing a review of this book that gives away the <u>assignment</u> part in the last section of the book! You can talk about the whole book except for the assignment. That would prevent other readers from getting the benefit of the experience! It's one thing to screw up the experience for yourself but quite another to do so for someone else.

Getting the Most from this Book

Here are a few instructions that will help you get the most from this book:

1. In the hope of making this book more experiential, you're encouraged to underline, write notes, and mark anything that stands out at you. Following this instruction is extremely important in creating more value than you'd otherwise get if you don't interact with the ideas in the book. If you feel strongly about anything, if you agree or disagree with anything, if any statement jumps out at you, please make sure to mark it somehow. You'll find out why later—it'll be well worth it. And when you find out the reason, remember that you can't share just that one part with anyone else until they've read the book themselves.

2. All readers aren't created alike, so there are two ways to read this book.
   a. For the more patient of readers, just read from the cover to cover.
   b. For the fast start reader wanting to get into the middle of the action, read it in this way:
      i. Start by reading section 2 on economic literacy.
      ii. Then read section 3 on capital management.
      iii. Then section 4 on productivity.
      iv. Then section 1 on entrepreneurship.

v. Then, only after you've read the first four sections, read the final section on wealth consciousness.

The Background

The following pages are made up of letters to my nephew Kidus (pronounced ki-deuce) who lives in Ethiopia. It's an attempt to teach him what he needs to know about how money (wealth) is made. It's my attempt to give him all the tools he needs to create a prosperous life if he comes to live in America. His father, sister, uncle (me) and his aunt (my sister) have all emigrated to the U.S. and there's a possibility he may join us soon.

He lives in Addis Ababa, the capital of Ethiopia. He speaks perfect English, has new paved roads (built by the Chinese), as well as clean water, food, but most importantly, Google and Youtube! Throughout the letters, sometimes I ask Kidus to watch a documentary or read an article online if he wants more background on a given topic. You may want to check them out as well.

Also, you may read some things you may not agree with in the following pages but keep going until the very last sentence and it will all make sense. Three small paragraphs may be hard to swallow for some (as they would've been for me at one time) but rest assured that it's part of the lesson.

A few reviewers of the book have said that, although they agreed with what they read, some of the stuff wasn't easy to stomach. For me, knowing the truth is important even if it's not what I want to hear or creates temporary discomfort. Keep in mind that experiencing a little temporary 'intellectual' pain will save you from experiencing *financial* pain. All our assumptions (i.e., our worldview) have consequences; our *economic* assumptions have financial consequences. Also remember that you can profit from every 'comfortable' or 'uncomfortable' idea in this book. Don't be discouraged about anything you learn; just remember that these ideas can be *monetized*.

Lastly, you may find it hard to believe that understanding economics can be so simple. But don't think that because it has been made easy, the quality has been diminished in any way. I take my readers very seriously. This book is as useful for someone who has a financial background as it is for the newbie.

In Your Service,
Akinaw Bulcha.

Adventures In Squirrelmerica

Dear Kidus,

I'm optimistic you can learn all you need to know about money, investing and wealth creation in a few short letters. My optimism isn't based on my teaching ability but on the fact that a little reflection on the current economic crisis can teach us all we need to know.

To make learning those lessons easier and more memorable, I've come up with a short story that we'll revisit from time to time. This story teaches three important things:

1. The big picture of how wealth is created in an economy.
2. The big picture of how wealth is destroyed.
3. The big picture of why the U.S. is in a recession.

"I found the crown of France in the gutter and picked it up." ~Napoleon.

Adventures in Squirrelmerica

"What a good country or a good squirrel should be doing is stashing away nuts for the winter. The United States is not only not saving nuts, it's eating the ones left over from the last winter." ~Bill Gross.

Imagine that America was a land of squirrels. The only thing Squirrelmerica bought and sold were nuts of all varieties.

Our story begins...

Since its founding, Squirrelmerica had gone through ups and downs, a civil war, unrest, and a global war on Communism. But it kept chugging along, always creating more prosperity for the next generation. Every generation left more nuts stashed away in the hollows of the forest trees for young Squirrelmericans to enjoy.

But in the 20th century, a strange virus slowly infected Squirrelmericans, distorting their ability to make good decisions. The virus silently drifted through the dense nut forest without the knowledge of the squirrels. The trees began to mysteriously produce more nuts than ever before all on their own. Enormous harvests magically appeared. This seemed like good news but Squirrelmericans didn't realize they were under a curse—a magician, one of their own, had found a way to make it look like there were more nuts on trees than there really were.

It seemed like good news at first but it was slowly leading them down the road to nutconomic collapse. But it was not their nutconomy alone that would suffer. Their spirits would also suffer.

As drops of acid slowly corrode even the strongest metals, so the magician's spell slowly ate away at the spirit of the once brave, proud squirrels. Slowly, and without their notice, they became squirrels without integrity, pride or a strong work ethic. Having been transformed by the slow degradation of their minds, they became sicklier and cowardly—as C.S. Lewis would put it, "They became squirrels without chests".

Their priorities changed from saving to spending, from earning to entitlements, from peace to war and from work to idleness.

Because of the squirrelagician's curse, Squirrelmericans carelessly ate way more nuts than they needed. Every squirrel was extremely fat and happy—they'd just lived through an incredible nut party that had lasted 25 years. When they gorged themselves and couldn't eat any more, they threw away perfectly good nuts. In fact, they became so wasteful, they used their edible nuts to build yachts, giant screen TVs, mansions and skyscrapers. They bought giant cars called NUTS-UVs that consumed a great deal of nutsoline to run.

The Causes of the Nutconomic Recession

Throughout the party years, no one realized they weren't planting new nut trees. Because the new trees seemed to mysteriously produced nuts all on their own, the squirrels stopped thinking of the future.

"The trees are blessed with strange magic, we need not work nor think of tomorrow!" they said. So, the party just kept roaring along; no one noticed the coming nutconomic catastrophe. Because they expected the magic to continue to work, Squirrelmericans doubled their rate of consumption and waste.

After eating all the nuts they had available, they devoured the nuts their parents and grandparents had saved up over the past 200 years (since the founding of Squirrelmerica when the first Squirrelitans arrived on Plymouth Nut).

After their nut inheritance was gone, they borrowed nuts from Chinese squirrels. For some reason, the Chinese squirrels were willing to eat much less, (and almost suffer hunger) in order to lend Squirrelmericans more nuts to consume.

After Squirrelmerica ate up *all* of its saved nuts, *all* of its nut inheritance and *all* of its borrowed nuts, a long, deep winter then set in. Then tragedy struck, the squirrelagician's potion stopped working. Squirrelmericans finally understood that the squirrelagician was a fraud and that the magic was a curse in disguise. As the weeks turned to months, Squirrelmerica's citizens began to shiver in the cold and moan of hunger.

A great deal of anger was stirring in the forest as the suffering intensified. The unemployment rate was 20%, 40 million squirrels were on nut stamps and millions more turned to peanut kitchens to stay alive. Inhabitants joined protest groups such as nut militias and nut parties to give voice to their anger, to demand change.

The Proposed Fix

Squirreliticians on Nutcapital Hill became alarmed and quickly turned to their secret weapon to alleviate the pain (and to save their furs)—the money printing press. "No need to fear", said their central banker Ben Squirrelnanke, "we'll keep printing nutty money (Squirrel Dollars) to avoid hunger and cold." Its government also continued to borrow money from every other squirrel nation in order to stimulate the nutconomy.

Now, when trillions of dollars of nutty money entered the nutconomy, do you think more nuts (wealth) were created as a result? Was food more available? Of course not!

All Squirrelnanke and the Acorn Treasury did by flooding the nutconomy with nutty money was to increase the ratio of dollars to nuts, *not nuts to squirrels*. No more wealth was created because no more nut trees were planted, nor nut factories built.

Sadly, when Squirrelmericans finally saw the importance of saving and investment in their nutconomy, they found they couldn't do so! The nutconomy had changed. When a lot of extra nuts (savings) *were* available, they could've invested in better factories and more fruitful nut trees. Doing so would've resulted in a surplus of nuts (wealth). But they decided to party instead when they had the chance to build a brighter future. After all, thanks to their great Squirrelagician, Alan Squirrelspan, *they had no idea they were over-consuming their nuts* (capital)—they thought they were eating from a real surplus, from a miraculous and bountiful harvest.

But now, all available nuts must be used for survival (what economists call present consumption); it's something Squirrelmericans call 'living from nutcheck to nutcheck'.

But there's something much more heartbreaking about what's now happening to Squirrelmericans. They've had to incur a massive amount of debt to pay for living expenses.

Because of money mismanagement, even while they go hungry, they must now pay $300 billion per year in interest to foreign squirrels who lent them money. All the borrowed money didn't create any more nuts. They're in a bigger hole now than ever before.

Will Squirrelmerica learn about what ails it or will it disintegrate? Only time will tell…

As I explain the principles of wealth creation in the following letters, remember this story because it teaches us almost all we need to know about it.

Also, please mark anything that stands out at you. You've been given an assignment that only requires you to do that one thing—you'll find out why later.

Your Loving Uncle,
  Akinaw.

Wealthology

Dear Kidus,

Not long after the worldwide recession began in 2007, the developing world was back on its feet, growing at an astounding rate. But America hasn't seen a real recovery yet. Thirty million Americans are still jobless or underemployed. Many Squirrelmericans want to know what happened, why it's happening, why the recovery is taking so long and what will happen in the future.

The millions who have lost their homes, jobs, and healthcare benefits are trying to make sense of the economic situation. They're asking why.

When we ask why, we're looking for causes. If we ask, "Why are so many people unemployed?" we're really asking a different question without realizing it: "What's the cause of wealth creation?" Jobs, after all, are gained or lost as the total available wealth in the economy expands or contracts.

Answering that one question would tell the business owner, investor, worker, student, and retiree what they need to know about their nutconomic system. After all, we're all after the same thing—to increase the total available wealth in the system.

The Problem With Reason

It's easy enough for a nation of squirrels to understand that deforestation contracts the supply of nuts in their nutconomy. They can all agree that in order to increase their wealth (nuts), more nut trees must be cultivated.

But something happens to the reasoning faculties of humans that complicates an otherwise simple concept. Unlike squirrels (to whom their nutconomy is simple to grasp) we humans have different theories of wealth creation. But should we have various theories of how food gets into our bellies? How can that be? Why has understanding nut creation turned into a paradox, a mystery?

We must answer that question, not only to increase the wealth in the system through our collective work (such as voting) but also to increase what we've got in our own pockets.

In attempting to answer the "wealth paradox", we should include one other question many look to answer during times of economic turbulence: How do you make it last? What causes *lasting* wealth? Many who've lost their jobs,

7

who've folded their businesses, want to avoid experiencing the bitter taste of impermanent prosperity. Many still find it unbelievable that so many giant, solid corporations can go bankrupt seemingly overnight.

When I worked for Citigroup over 13 years ago, it was a solid, giant financial empire with almost $1 trillion dollars in assets. But just a little over a decade later, it was borrowing hundreds of billions of dollars just to stay afloat. What caused this enormous change in its fortune?

As an entrepreneur I asked myself these questions, but it wasn't until the present financial meltdown began and intensified, that all the pieces finally came together (you'll understand why later). I instantly understood everything very clearly.

(The biggest clue in understanding how recessions are made is to answer this one question: "What's the one thing that connects all nutconomic activity together?" If our *entire* nutconomy implodes all at once, the cause must be common to all our economic activities. Something in our nutconomy has "*collectivized*" our successes and failures. It's up to you to find out what it is as you read on).

Not only did I finally understand the causes of recessions and wealth creation, but I had also learned the mind habits and principles that must be cultivated in order to build and maintain a financially prosperous life. In the blink of an eye, my prosperity consciousness was changed forever.

As we explore these principles, we must remember that the path to victory is clearest in times of defeat. The present economic situation will give us as much as we choose to take away from it. Theologians tell us that were it not for sin, we couldn't know God's mercy. The romantic tells us that were it not for absence, the heart would not grow fond.

In the realm of money, business and economics, *we can learn much more in the absence of excess prosperity (after the nut trees have been deforested) than we could in the midst of it.*

If we're ready, open and willing, experience is a great teacher. So what did my experience teach me about creating lasting wealth?

A: That anyone (or society) who wants to create lasting wealth must master four principles: *Entrepreneurship, Economic Literacy, Capital Management and Productivity.* Whenever wealth is created or destroyed, it results from the use or avoidance of these four principles.

"I always wanted to be somebody, but now I realize I should have been more specific"
~Lily Tomlin.

8

Be Wealthy, Don't be Rich

You can become rich by using a single principle, but if you don't learn and use all four together, you won't have lasting wealth.

There's a big difference between being rich and being wealthy. Contrary to popular belief, few people can become rich while just about everyone can become wealthy. Being rich depends on circumstance, luck, constant work or a natural ability which usually shows up as a single, dominant trait.

Wealth, on the other hand, is a result of "wealth consciousness", an accurate understanding of how we squirrels really make our nuts. You may call it economics but the idea of teaching you economics is as depressing to me as it might be to you. Economics today is an anemic, haphazard and dishonest profession. Such dishonesty is made plain in that there are different "schools of economics."

Wading through the charlatans, government bureaucrats and Wall Street sponsored economists has required a considerable amount of work, time and money. *You can bypass the idiocy, dishonesty and confusion I had to swim through to get a clear understanding of money, prosperity and economics by reading my letters.*

"If a man empties his purse into his head, no one can take it from him."
~Benjamin Franklin.

What is Wealth?

It's important that we define wealth since these four principles are designed to create it. I define wealth as owning assets that produce an amount of income that's greater than your living expenses.

Financial freedom depends on passive, positive cash flow—but that must start from within. It's a product of mind and heart. You can't have positive cash flow unless you learn how to be an entrepreneur, *how to* manage your capital, *how to* be productive and *how to* think like a good nutconomist.

"Son, if you really want something in this life, you have to work for it. Now quiet! They're about to announce the lottery numbers." ~Homer Simpson

It's Easy to Learn but...

Once wealth consciousness is understood, the process of becoming wealthy will be easier because you'll understand the only principles that produce lasting wealth. You'll be able to explain market conditions, see opportunities and dangers without having to rely on biased advisers, nutconomists or greedy brokers.

Sadly, we live in a dishonest world. Modern squirrels use their intellect as a weapon in much the same way prehistoric ones used spears or swords to kill enemies. We're still savages, people are still brutal—the only difference is that, in prehistoric times, identifying your enemy was simpler. In today's world, politics and marketing has perfected the art of getting people to do things that are not in their best interest by concealing information, obscuring reality, appealing to fear or making veiled threats.

Here's an example. While doing some research, I came across this quote on the U.S. Treasury's website: "The United States debt, foreign and domestic, was the price of liberty." Here's what the Treasury is really saying: "If you want to keep your freedom, you better let us do what we want with your money. If you don't let us run up huge debts, you'll be at risk of losing everything you've got, all that you love and hold dear."

This appeal to freedom through voluntary enslavement works like magic in Squirrelmerica as it does elsewhere. As soon as our governments tell people it's fighting for freedom, the free, dissenting, independent, spirit recoils into a fetal position and dies. The air out of dissent is miraculously let out and people fall in line, even becoming cheerleaders in their own demise.

It's no wonder America's always at war—the War on Communism, the War on Poverty, the War on Drugs, the War on Terror, etc. Government has found a button in all of us that can be pushed to get us to do what it wants. Propaganda works with *our* minds, with *our* ideas and the fears *we* harbor inside. The source of all our problems resides in our hearts.

So as easy as it is to understand wealth consciousness, we make it more difficult than it has to be. But we must not judge ourselves for failing to understand the economy. Understanding it is also difficult because the economics profession is dishonest.

"Courage is not simply one of the virtues, but the form of every virtue at the testing point."
~C.S. Lewis.

The Rules of Adding Still Apply!

Our central bank (the Federal Reserve) has done something quite fascinating—it's actually convinced the American people that the rules of adding and subtracting they learned in 1ˢᵗ grade don't apply to the field of economics. Their "distinguished" economists tell us "deficits don't matter."

But if deficits don't matter, neither do profits, since profits are just the flip side of deficits. And if neither deficits nor surpluses matter, why should anyone work? Why don't we just print $1 million, hand it to every American and be done with it?

To understand a bit more about the Federal Reserve propaganda machine, search for an online article entitled, "Priceless: How the Federal Reserve Bought the Economics Profession". This is the crazy, truth confiscating and truth suffocating environment you may be coming into Kidus.

A lot of people in Squirrelmerica feel like tiny ships in turbulent, stormy nutconomic waters. Unfortunately, all the captains and navigators happen to be drunk. Instead of navigating away from financial storms, they head directly into the midst of the very storm they've helped create. After reading what I've got to say in the following letters, you'll no longer feel like a tiny ship lost in the sea of global capitalism without knowing where to dock your little boat, what to do with your money.

I once also felt lost in deep, dark nutconomic waters. Like many others lately, I see that the American political and economic system isn't only dishonest but also incompetent even *if* their intentions are good.

The average American doesn't know, for example, about a secret tax that eats up anywhere between 6 to 9% of their income every single year. They may not know about it because they don't understand what money is or how it works. This is why they need to build the principles of capital management and economic literacy.

There's a way to avoid this secret tax but first, we must *know* it's there to begin with; all economic and financial inequality rests on our own ignorance and a lack of self-confidence in our ability to make good financial decisions.

The secret tax is just one way the system is unfair *if* we're unaware of how it works. In fact, we can even use the unfairness and deceit of the nutconomic system to our own benefit. Education has the habit of turning every pessimist into an optimist. When it comes to financial matters, ignorance isn't bliss. Every nutconomic system (except pure capitalism) is, in part, rigged to benefit some at the expense of others.

The nut making process doesn't have to be a mystery if you allow it not to be so. We must be willing to give up control of what we think we know to learn something new. We must give up any preconceived ideas about money and the wealth building process. Willful ignorance brings us only one thing: A state of virtual nonexistence. We can only truly exist, if we do so in truth. We can only be prosperous if we believe the right assumptions.

"A gap in our awareness is a gap in our existence." ~Anonymous.

How it Works: A Story

Let me explain the importance of using these four principles together through a story.

We know that some squirrels can get rich through natural ability, luck, perseverance or an innate entrepreneurial sense. But they may lose the money they've made using their entrepreneurial skill if they haven't learned some of the other skills. They may be able to start the wealth creation process but unable to sustain it. Singer Toni Braxton is a great example of this fast-start, slow financial death scenario. Our world is filled with plenty of people who come into some money but end up losing it all in a surprisingly short amount of time.

One good entrepreneur (true story—you'll learn his identity when we revisit the story), for example, made over $100 million in the computer software business. His entrepreneurial ability earned him an enormous amount of money. But in a few short years, his fortune dropped to $4 million. Why did he lose $96 million?

He lost his fortune because he lacked *economic literacy*. Without knowing it, he had crossed over into a different industry when he got into real estate.

Computer software and real estate are two *very* different industries. Economic literacy would have pointed out *how* they were different (it's not what you think it is). Knowing the difference could've saved this entrepreneur $96 million. Now that you see the value, I hope you'll pay attention. I wish someone had taught me these things when I first arrived in Squirrelmerica from Squirrelthopia.

Your Loving Uncle,
    Akinaw.

Part One

*The Secrets
of Entrepreneurship*

The Only Way
Money is Made

Dear Kidus,

As a child living in the outskirts of Ethiopia, I remember dreaming about what Squirrelmerica was like. I grew up thinking it was a land of opportunity where you could create a free, prosperous life if you worked hard for it. After having lived here for decades, I've got a more holistic understanding of nutconomics. I've learned three important things about creating prosperity in the Squirrelmerican economic system.

Hard Work is Penalized

First, you can forget about becoming rich through hard work.

The hard work gospel is taught from elementary school through college but it's an outdated gospel. Squirrelmerica is still the land of opportunity but only for the squirrels who know how to work smart. Hard work can no longer give Americans the same quality of life previous generations experienced. Nowadays it takes two squirrels working outside the tree to afford the same nuts prior generations used to enjoy with one working squirrel.

Smart work, in my view, consists of one thing—knowing how an economic system creates and destroys wealth (knowing the rules).

One of these rules is that our economic system actually penalizes hard work. America's middle class, for example, pay a much larger percentage of their incomes in taxes than the wealthiest squirrels in our forests. A little economic investigation would reveal the rules used by the wealthy can be used by anyone else. Income inequality is always self imposed through an alliance with ignorance.

Everything has a price, and if you're willing to pay the same price others have paid to get what they've got, you'll get those things too. Paying the price for financial freedom starts with education and ends with experience; initially, it takes a lot of reading, experimenting, courage and study.

"I am looking for a lot of men who have an infinite capacity to not know what can't be done."
~Henry Ford.

15

The Will to Let Go

Secondly, I've learned that even if people realize that outdated ideas don't serve their financial interests, they're unwilling to let go of them.

Immigrants like us have the advantage of being pragmatic. Our goal is to create the prosperity we wouldn't have had, had we not come to Squirrelmerica. It's difficult to grow up without paved roads or plumbing and not want to take advantage of the opportunity in front of us. Growing up in the Ethiopian countryside, we didn't have $100 pairs of Air Jordans—we just had *air*; we had no shoes.

"Courage is contagious. When a brave man takes a stand, the spines of others are often stiffened." ~Billy Graham.

Appeal to Authority Works

Thirdly, I've seen that Squirrelmericans are subjected to a deafening chorus of financial and economic experts who are either *really* incompetent, insincere or paid propagandists for special interests. Economists generally have two clients—Wall Street and the Federal Government. The Wall Street/government propaganda machine works like magic.

For example, the other day I was watching a financial news network with a friend. An economist from a prestigious university was talking about the state of the economy. When he said something a five year old could understand to be complete nonsense, I said, "I can't believe this guy is saying this, he's out of his mind."

Immediately after I said that my friend replied, "He can't be wrong, he teaches at Berkley." I was astounded that he'd give credence to complete nonsense although he knew very little about economics. A lot of people who listened to these experts are now experiencing a lot of hurt, pain, sorrow and anxiety.

We must forget all we've learned or heard about money (and the experts we heard it from) in order to build a new foundation for lasting wealth. We must ignore the human temptation to give in to authority.

"A learned man has always riches in himself." ~The Phaedrus.

The Principle of Entrepreneurship

Of the major economic ideas we must relearn, entrepreneurship is at the top of the list. Eighty five percent of people who have become millionaires did so by owning their own business. Nine out of the top ten billionaires on Forbes magazine's yearly ranking had entrepreneurial parents.

The *art of entrepreneurship* is our path to success. Learning how to be a nutpreneur is your gateway to financial freedom. Without learning this skill, you can't be prosperous. There's no other way to become financially free, vacation around the world, or retire early.

The other skills I mentioned (capital management, economic literacy and productivity) only serve to apply this initial starting point.

"It's true hard work never killed anybody, but I figure, why take the chance?"
~Ronald Reagan.

How Entrepreneurs Make Money

Whether we're investors, wage workers, or business owners, we all do the same thing; if anyone plans or makes decisions, that person is an entrepreneur. If you plan to work for someone else, you're using entrepreneurial skills to decide whom to work for. If you manage your own money, you're an entrepreneur because you put your money where you expect growth.

If someone else manages your money for you, you're still an entrepreneur because you expect the person to whom you outsource money decisions to grow the value of your portfolio. So what's the definition of an entrepreneur?

It's this: *Nutpreneurs are in the business of forecasting future nut crops.* We make decisions today based on where we think the market will be tomorrow. Everyone does this guessing consciously or unconsciously. Those who do it consciously make more money than those who don't. All human motivation is based on a guess, a promise that if we go through a series of steps, if we perform certain acts, we'll get something for it when we're done. Dogs only do tricks if they can expect a treat.

We may go our whole lives without being aware we get paid to predict; but that's all we get paid for. Entrepreneurs don't get paid for physical work, they get paid to think, predict, and calculate.

"Prepare your work outside and make it ready for yourself in the field; afterwards, then, build your house" ~Proverbs 24:7.

Seeing in the Dark

You can learn a lot about life at the gym. You can, for example, understand just how competitive guys can be.

One of my most memorable gym experiences was when this huge bodybuilder, who must've had self esteem the size of a pea, was groaning like he was having a baby every time he picked up weights. I mean it was so loud, people were looking at each other wondering what his issue was. When it comes to competition, guys can do some dumb things.

In the realm of business, there's a lot more on the line than just losing face—you can lose a lot of money if you're not competitive. Our definition of entrepreneurs as forecasters helps us understand how to be competitive. Being able to predict what others can't—being able to see what others don't, is the meaning of being *competitive.*

In general this ability pays off big. I once heard someone say that Warren Buffett was just one of those people "who can see in the dark". There aren't that many people who can see in the dark. That's why those who can are paid a lot of money. Your job as an entrepreneur is to develop the best night vision goggles you can find.

"You'll see it when you believe it." ~Dr. Wayne Dyer.

A $600 Million Business Lesson

Successful people ask questions others aren't willing to ask and they're sometimes ridiculed for doing so. No matter how difficult it may be, you must get in the habit of being an independent thinker. Only independent thinkers can remain flexible to changes that take place in the world of business and adapt.

I once briefly talked with the founder of the 99 cent stores. I shook the hands that built a fortune of $600 million and asked, "Do you have any words of advice for a young entrepreneur?" Without hesitating, he looked at me with a smile and said, "Just do something other people aren't doing." That's the kind of mentality that pays off big.

He's saying that we're not the only forecasters in business. Other entrepreneurs also make bets on where they think the market's headed.

If you want to start a new business, the amount of money you make depends on whether other people are thinking the same thing. If everyone else knows about a good fishing spot and more fishermen show up, there'll be fewer fish to go around. Opportunities can be discounted. Your job is to find a new fishing spot before the word's out and rent space to others when it's found out.

That's another way of saying you must be a *contrarian* thinker to be wildly successful. A contrarian thinker is someone like Warren Buffett. One of his investment principles, is to "be fearful when others are greedy and to be greedy when others are fearful". That way of thinking guarantees that he'll find only the unspoiled fishing holes.

"Take calculated risks. That is quite different from being rash." ~George Patton.

Natural Selection Principle

Have you ever wondered why some people are more successful than others? Why do some companies make it? Why do others fail? There's a simple answer to that.

Entrepreneurs who make accurate predictions earn more money. Entrepreneurs who keep making lousy predictions end up working for the better predictors. There's a kind of "natural selection" process that weeds out the good predictors from the bad ones.

Many people want to work for themselves, set their own hours, and become financially free in our society. What they may not know is that the only thing separating them from their boss is forecasting ability (smart work).

"The secret of success is to know something nobody else knows." ~Aristotle Onassis.

Investors are Entrepreneurs

One of the best ways to become financially independent is to be a good investor. But what makes someone a good investor?

We've answered that question: Good investors are good entrepreneurs. They're just *passive* entrepreneurs. Instead of working for money, they have their money work for them.

Even if we're not independent investors, we're still paying someone else to do the predicting and are therefore still making an educated guess on how well that money manager will do. We're outsourcing the role of a

19

nutpreneur. Money managers and investment advisers make bets in your place. That's all they get paid for.

"Decision is a risk rooted in the courage of being free." ~Paul Tillich.

A Billion Dollar Blackjack Lesson

Bill Gross is a well known, respected money manager; he's become a billionaire because of his ability to make good bets.

He regularly appears on CNBC and Bloomberg; he's quoted by numerous financial publications, followed by thousands of investors and he manages one of the biggest bond funds in the world. He lives in a beautiful $23 million Newport Beach mansion. It's good to be Bill Gross. How did Bill gain all this fame, respect, and wealth?

Bill began his illustrious career by making bets in a casino. He was a professional blackjack player before he began his career as a money manager—it was in a casino that he learned how to make bets and spread risk.

"Risk comes from not knowing what you're doing." ~Warren Buffett.

How Warren Does It

Let's take a look at one American I admire. How does, Warren Buffett, the greatest investor of all time, make his bets? Of the top ten billionaires on Forbes magazine's annual list, Buffett is the only one to have made his money from investing.

I came across a book titled, *"The Warren Buffett Way: Investment Strategies of the World's Greatest Investor"* that helped me understand how he invests. We can get a glimpse just by reading the forward written by legendary money manager Peter Lynch:

- Warren looks for investments with as little risk as possible.
- He's very good at understanding probability and being a great oddsmaker.
- According to Lynch, Warren's a good oddsmaker for three reasons: 1) a love of math computations, 2) a devotion to the game of bridge, and 3) a lifetime's worth of experience in underwriting risk in his insurance and reinsurance businesses.

- Warren only takes risks if the odds of complete loss are nil and when potential gain is significant.

Lynch's explanation reinforces what we've been saying all along: The most successful people on earth are great *oddsmakers*, educated economic guessers. They're brain workers.

"If we do what is necessary, all the odds are in our favor." ~Charles Buxton.

The Best Way to Make a Good Bet

Clearly understanding the role of a nutpreneur as a forecaster of future nut demand helps us hedge our bets. Let's assume we want to manage our own investments. What stocks should we buy? What industry? Cashews? Almonds? Peanuts?

The answer is in industries in which we can best make a good bet. We should stick with what we know best. All the great investors from Jim Rogers to Warren Buffett say this same thing continuously. The simpler an investment, the better our odds that we'll win because there's less to know about it; we reduce the risk of losing money because we can better understand where that market is headed.

"An investment in knowledge always pays the best interest." ~Benjamin Franklin.

Workers are Entrepreneurs

I repeatedly tell my students wage workers *are* entrepreneurs. When I assign a business plan, someone in my class will say, "But I don't want to own my business."

But workers make bets too. Their bet is that their company (or industry) will be around for awhile. They're also betting that the company they wish to work for will pay well. Different jobs have different potential.

Throughout most of my life, Microsoft has not only paid some of the highest wages in the country but has also created over 2,000 millionaires. Microsoft employees made the bet that enrolling in computer technology programs in college, working for a tech startup and trading wages for stock options would lead to a life of financial abundance.

21

Squirrelmericans mistakenly believe we can escape the risks of nutpreneurship. In the hope of avoiding risk, they get jobs without realizing they're taking on *more* risk. After all, wage workers don't learn the higher aspects of making money. Learning how to make money doesn't happen overnight. The learning process takes awhile but the sooner we get started the better.

Workers have the disadvantage of *not* learning how to make money on the job, the worker just stands still. We must never stand still, we must empower ourselves by accumulating all the necessary knowledge, experience and skills we need to create a prosperous life.

"Before everything else, getting ready is the secret to success." ~Henry Ford.

Case Study: Kirk Kerkorian

Stories help us understand what a million words can't. Let's see how the law of entrepreneurship (prediction) plays out in the real world. The story of billionaire investor Kirk Kerkorian is a great illustration.

After serving as a pilot in World War II, Kerkorian came back to the states and stuck with what he knew—he got into the airline business. Just as Las Vegas was starting to develop, he started his career as a pilot, transporting California gamblers to casinos.

After years of saving, he noticed demand for flights was growing. So he started his own airline. At the time, commercial aviation was a new and growing business. When he bought a small airline company for $60,000, he made a bet that the industry would grow.

He was right. 20 years later, he sold the airline business for $104 million. Then he made another bet that paid off big. He looked around and saw that the casino business was growing. So he started to buy up land on the Strip, the most famous and valuable part of Las Vegas. One lot cost him about $1 million. By renting the space to a casino operator, he ended up netting $9 million per year from that one lot alone.

As he learned a little bit more about the casino business, he put up his own casinos on the lots he'd bought. In 1986, he sold some of his casinos for about $600 million.

"If a window of opportunity appears, don't pull down the shade. ~Thomas J. Peters

How Kerkorian Created His Fortune

Nothing about Kerkorian's story is strange or unbelievable. Luck only played a part in that he served as an airline pilot in World War II.

The gamblers who flew on Kerkorian's planes saw the same casinos, the same economic development and the same Strip he did. Many of these people were probably Hollywood movie stars who had the money to buy a piece of the strip at the time. But they didn't.

Opportunities are all about us. We need only start where we are, with what we know most about, notice trends and start making predictions. We can all make good bets with practice. In fact, we can make better bets than the Wall Street analysts who do it for a living.

I remember reading a book written by the famous fund manager Peter Lynch titled, *"One up on Wall Street."* His main point was that the average investor has a decisive edge on Wall Street because we can see trends rising from the ground, from the street. We're closer to the action.

"Opportunity is often difficult to recognize; we usually expect it to beckon us with beepers and billboards." ~William Arthur Ward.

How to Look at Failure

Experienced entrepreneurs know how to make failure pay because they're the only group of people who understand what it is.

Failure just teaches us that the bet we've made wasn't based on good assumptions. Failure shows us what didn't work and in that way, brings us closer to what will work. So, in reality, there's no such thing as failure. This isn't wishful thinking, it's accurate economic insight.

The famous inventor, Thomas Edison understood this because he failed thousands of times. His attitude was that every failure just showed him what didn't work and therefore, put him just one step closer to finding what did work.

This process of approximating your way to success explains the "magic of persistence." A lot of business coaches and motivational speakers preach this idea of persistence but usually don't explain *why* it pays off.

Persistence is not doing the same thing repetitively expecting a different result—that's the definition of insanity. Persistence makes you a better entrepreneur by building your forecasting ability. If one plan doesn't work, try another. With every plan, we get closer to our basket of nuts. That's why persistence is so valuable.

When I failed at different business ventures in the past, I didn't learn everything I could've learned because I didn't have a conscious and accurate concept of entrepreneurship. But now that I have a clear concept of it, I know what to do with *prior* failures. I can make failure pay.

"He who never made a mistake never made a discovery." ~Samuel Smiles.

Conversation with a Venture Capitalist

Lenders to business startups know the value of failure. I once talked to a vice president of a venture capital firm based in Canada about how they figure out whom to lend money to. "So do you guys basically use credit scores?" I asked.

"No, we don't care about credit so much," he replied. I was confused—in the world of real estate, credit scores are the biggest of factors.

"So you guys must rely heavily on assets then."

"No, not as much as you may think."

"So what's left? Do their pets have to co-sign for the loan?" I asked.

He laughed and said, "Actually, one of the biggest requirements we have for lending money is that the person applying must have failed at a prior business."

"Failure is nature's plan to prepare you for great responsibilities." ~Napoleon Hill.

How to Make Failure Pay

The key to learning from failure is to let it speak—to give it a voice. Most people mistakenly think that failure is just something to "get over" or a hurdle to get past, so they become ashamed of it.

When we feel ashamed of failure, we lose what benefit we could've received from it. If you think about it accurately, the only failures in life are those who *don't* fail. I urge you, therefore, to start experimenting if you make it to Squirrelmerica or stay in Squirrelthopia.

Experiencing an economic depression at a young age has been the luckiest break of my life. As a result, I've learned a great deal about entrepreneurial calculation—the gateway to enduring, meaningful prosperity.

"Failure is in a sense the highway to success, as each discovery of what is false leads us to seek earnestly after what is true." ~John Keats.

The Greatest Gift

Based on what I've said, you should be able to figure out why the current nutconomic recession is the best thing that could've happened to our generation, a fortune in disguise for investors, entrepreneurs, voters—for everybody. See if you can figure it out.

Here's a hint: "Truth sooner emerges from error than confusion." – Borden P. Bowne. Here's a bigger hint: Systematic economic truth is more easily found in the aftermath of systematic economic errors.

Remember, although it's generally thought entrepreneurs take risks, they're actually people who progressively eliminate risk, and as they do, their profits increase. Knowing this will help you understand everything else about the economy.

Your Loving Uncle,
    Akinaw

26

The Rules of the
Money Game

Dear Kidus,

Every day, we're faced with life and death decisions. When a man hears, "Does this dress make me look fat?" he's on the edge of ruin. Of course, no man in his right mind would say, "Kind of" or "*just* a tad". But even if he says, "No, of course not", he's got to make it *believable*. And guess what? A man never knows if he'll succeed in making it believable and like Russian roulette, he may only have one chance at getting it right.

Fortunately making money is a lot more predictable and you get more than one chance. As I've said, being an entrepreneur requires that we risk making mistakes. Making money is an *approximating* process. The rules I've outlined below are designed to make the process of making money a bit shorter.

"During the first period of a man's life the greatest danger is not to take the risk."
~Soren Kierkegaard.

Rule #1: Learn from History

When deciding to make a certain investment, start a new business or a new career, it's important to remember that history always repeats itself.

Our financial status is just the total or *cumulative* effects of past decisions; the *present* is really the *past*, today's circumstances are really the result of yesterday's choices. What we see, hear, know and experience is really an echo of the past.

In order to learn the financial lessons history has to teach us Squirrelmericans, we need to ask this question: "Which *types* of financial principles produce a prosperous life and which ones create a life of poverty?" All you must do then is follow the principles that work and avoid the ones that don't.

Whether you want to be a great investor, fashion designer, actor, industrialist, lawyer or anything else, you can best learn how to do it right by finding out what others have done to gain their success. There's no need to reinvent the wheel.

27

"Experience is the school of mankind, and they will learn at no other." ~Edmund Burke

The Ghost in History's Machine

So how do we learn from history? How can we become better nutpreneurs using this rule? People give lip service about learning from history but few understand how to do so.

If we want to learn from other people's successes and failures, we want to look at the *ideas* that caused them to succeed or fail. Don't look *at* successful people, look *past* them. If it's been done before, it can be done again. Some falsely believe that those who have experienced dramatic success are either "just smart" or they're "go-getters". When I tell my students selling is a necessary business skill, I'll invariably hear someone say, "But I'm not the sales type".

I dislike that word "just" because it tells me the people who use it don't want to change. The truth is, nothing *just* happens—everything has a cause and when looking to learn from the past, you want to look at causes. The causes of either success or failure are always ideas, thoughts. Learning from history is, therefore, tracing the consequences of thoughts or ideas.

One of the best ways to learn from history is to learn as much as we can about successful people we want to be like. We want to know enough about our heroes to get inside their heads, to pick their brains, and to even joke and argue with them as if they were your buddy. And once we understand as much as we can about them, before making a big financial decision, ask ourselves, "What would they do?"

I read biographies of successful business people I respect in order to acquire the ideas and habits that have made them successful. This is something all successful squirrels do. Warren Buffett, for example, read the biographies of all the great captains of industry from Carnegie to Vanderbilt early on in his life.

If you go on YouTube.com, you can find a five part speech he gave to MBA students in which he says that all we must do to be successful is look at what people we admire have done and just copy them. People, like animals, learn by imitation. The opportunities the hand of history has dealt, it will deal again. Our job is to be ready to put time tested ideas to use the next time we're given an opportunity that resembles something that's happened to someone else before.

I'll finish this rule with this: I've read lots of books and listened to lots of experts on success—almost all of them stress the importance of having great people guide our lives. Great people are great *ideas*—nothing more, nothing less.

Ideas, like viruses, can inhabit the bodies of different people—they are *transpersonal.*

In the words of one of my favorite philosophers, "A person is a proposition." All you must do to get the life you want is to think the thoughts great people have thought.

"A man is but the product of his thoughts, what he thinks, he becomes." ~Ghandi.

Rule #2: Master Luck

The second tool the entrepreneur can use to make good decisions is to master luck. This idea of mastering luck, as you'll see, is based on understanding how history unfolds.

One of the main reasons I'm interested in psychology, history and nutconomics is that I've noticed *early adaptation to big historical trends is one of the most important factors that make people very successful in a relatively short amount of time.* We must get into a habit of projecting big, historical movements.

Bill Gates was obviously an early adapter—he got into computers and software in high school before most of the world had ever heard the word, "personal computer". By the time he was 30 years old, his company was worth more than the McDonald's corporation, which brings me to my next example.

Ray Kroc, the founder of McDonald's Corporation, was also an early adapter in a less obvious way. Kroc's success resulted from the booming post-war economy, the baby boomer generation who became teenage fast food junkies and to increased mobility. More cars equaled more drive thru sales.

Twenty six years after Kroc's death, McDonald's has over 32,000 locations and serves at least a billion customers every month. He mastered luck and shows us all that getting swept up to success is a much simpler path to success than luck, hard work or experimentation.

Ray Kroc may not have been *conscious* of the historical factors that made him a giant success, but the leadership of the company he left behind does understand those factors. McDonald's is expanding in China just as the Chinese are going through the same mobility boom Squirrelmericans experienced after World War II. The only difference is that China is supersizing its mobility surge to the tune of 13 million cars per year.

Mastering luck requires an understanding of how history is unfolding from an opportunistic point of view. Before buying the McDonald's franchise, Ray Kroc saw growth in much the same way the casino magnate Kirk

Kerkorian noticed increased traffic in Las Vegas before he made a decision to buy land on the Strip. Small investors and entrepreneurs need to understand this concept.

"Nothing is so often irretrievably missed as a daily opportunity." ~Marie Eschenbach.

The Man Who Coined "Mastering Luck"

We repeatedly see great examples of historical figures that have literally been swept up to success. Of all those who have risen to greatness, Napoleon's rise has been the most dramatic and rapid. By the age of 30, he was the most powerful man in France. By the time he was 34, he was an Emperor; by the time he was 37, he ruled most of Europe. And if he had a navy to cross the English Channel, Napoleon would have been the first ruler since the ancient Caesars to establish a universal kingdom. How did he accomplish so much?

Although he was obviously a genius, he wasn't so vain as to say he'd done it all himself. *Genius needs help.* Napoleon said he was successful because he always "moved with the opinion of millions of people".

Napoleon's genius was his ability to recognize where people's ideas were heading and marching in front of them. He created the idea that he was *the* symbol and protector of the Revolution sweeping Europe, thereby *leveraging the energy of the movement to realize his own ambitions.*

He called that process "mastering luck". He said, "Great men become great because they've been able to master luck, but what the commoners call luck is a characteristic of genius."

Being a financial or business genius depends on your ability to master luck. When Warren Buffett buys stocks, he masters luck. He usually waits and watches a business until a crisis occurs before loading up on its stock. When he bought huge stakes in American Express decades ago, it was in the middle of a crisis. When he recently invested $5 billion in Goldman Sachs and billions more in other companies in the middle of a deep financial crisis, he was mastering luck.

Napoleon is saying that we're all lucky in some way because history gives us all a chance to become great at what we love if we open our eyes to opportunity.

"Ability is of little account without opportunity." ~Napoleon.

How to Master Luck: The Story of Bob Pelissier

Former truck driver Bob Pelissier understands how to master luck. I came across his story as I was reading the May 2010 edition of a newsletter from the Motley Fool. Here's a paraphrased version of the story:

On a muggy fall night in 1985, Bob Pelissier's life changed forever. It was nearly one in the morning, and the 56-year-old truck driver was flipping through the channels when he came across a late-night infomercial advertising "an unprecedented breakthrough in telecommunications."

Mildly intrigued, Bob listened as the announcer explained that something called a "cellular telephone" was about to "change the lifestyles of millions"—and that investing in this technology was the "business opportunity of the century."

At first, Bob was skeptical. But when he heard that AT&T predicted one day as much as 40% of all calls would come from cell phones, he slowly began to change his mind.

Now, you probably already know where I'm going with this, but I urge you to bear with me for just a moment longer...This story has a unique twist that could help *you* secure a small fortune. Exactly how much are we talking?

Well, had you invested just $5,000 in the little-known stock I'm going to tell you about today back when smartphones first hit the market, today you'd be sitting on as much as $295,000.

Nevertheless, you might be wondering if you wouldn't just be better off investing in a well-known giant like Apple or AT&T. Which brings me back to my original story...As you've probably guessed, Bob Pelissier and his wife, Lorraine, went on to retire multi-millionaires—despite the fact that he drove a big rig for the better part of four decades and she worked 12 hours a day selling sandwiches out of the back of a van.

And it probably comes as no surprise that dozens of other people just like Bob and Lorraine walked away with just as much -- if not more. But here's something that I'm pretty sure WILL surprise you...

These folks *didn't* invest in the companies that made cell phones... or even in the carriers that owned and operated the cellular networks.

Instead, they invested in something far less obvious--but far more valuable...You see, what they essentially ended up buying was the rights to the radio frequencies that cell phones use to make wireless phone calls (tech types call this "spectrum").

In fact, Bob Pelissier owned the rights for just two cities: Manchester and Nashua, New Hampshire. I realize that doesn't sound all that impressive. But, here's the thing...Had Bob invested in a company that made cell phones, the value of his

31

investment would have been directly tied to how many cell phones *that* company was able to sell.

Had he invested in a specific cellular carrier, it would have been directly tied to how many subscribers *that* carrier's network was able to attract—and let's not forget that the competition was just as fierce back then as it is today.

Meanwhile, *because all cell phones used the same radio frequencies,* the value of the spectrum Bob owned increased regardless of what cell phone brands people were buying or carriers they were choosing.

All that mattered was that more and more people were using cell phones all the time. In other words, it was the ultimate win-win wireless investment.

"All great work is preparing yourself for the accident to happen." ~Sidney Lumet.

Rule #3: Choose Your Environment Carefully

How much money we make and how fast we do it depends on the environment in which we choose to grow our investment. Like a good farmer, we want to plant our seeds in fertile soil. Certain economies, like types of soil, will produce very little while others will produce an abundant harvest.

One fertile patch of land where you can expect an abundant harvest is China. Now, I'm not optimistic about China's prospects because of its enormous population, its location or its past economic performance. I'm optimistic about China's economy because its culture was made for business.

Instead of borrowing and consuming, they save and invest like true capitalists. Chinese citizens as a group, *have more savings than any other economy in the world!* As you learn about nutconomics, you'll see why this fact is one of the biggest reasons China will be the biggest economy in the world much sooner than we realize.

Squirrelmerica's savings rate has been in the low single digits for a long time—it's even dipped below 0% (negative savings rate).

As the U.S. is mired in a huge mountain of debt, as Europe copes with its debt crisis, as California is on the brink of collapse, as our federal budget deficit has gone past $13 trillion, the Chinese government itself is sitting on a *surplus* of $2.5 trillion.

These people are serious, competent and they're extremely business minded. One of my students is Chinese and she tells me that "all they [Chinese] care about is making money". "Everyone," she said, "has a business of their own."

32

Her remarks remind me of one made by Napoleon who once said that Britain was "a nation of shopkeepers." Perhaps that's a sign that China will become a modern day British Empire. The British Empire expanded across the globe because they were obsessed with trade and commerce. Asian culture in general is *obsessed* with success. Squirrelmerican kids pay to sit next to the Asian students for a reason.

"A nation's culture resides in the hearts and in the soul of its people." ~Ghandi.

What We Don't See

The Chinese have another underrated asset—their foreign policy. Like its people, China's foreign policy is strangely peaceful, non-ideological and business friendly. Not getting wrapped up in international conflicts gives China a *huge* advantage in international commerce.

China's foreign policy is focused on creating friends and business relationships while ours is busy creating sanctions and enemies across the globe. When we create sanctions, it limits the places where American companies can do business while increasing China's areas of *exclusive* access.

If you were to invest in two companies, one that's created enemies and one that has none, which would you choose? Venezuela, Brazil, Iran, Saudi Arabia are fairly large, resource rich countries that are doing more business with China than with Squirrelmerica. It seems unbelievable that China, still only one third the size of our economy is doing more business with Brazil than we are!

The truth is, Latin American countries prefer to do business with China because of our heavy handed foreign policy in the past. China has never been an aggressive nation in their recent history.

America's obsession is to control, create sanctions and wage wars whereas the Chinese care only about one thing: *making money*. Here's the important thing about all of this: *The Chinese are building a good* <u>*brand*</u>*—that of a friendly superpower.* A pragmatic investor would invest in an economy that's expanding commerce and creating friends rather than reducing its opportunities abroad.

"The laziest man I ever met put popcorn in his pancakes so they would turn over by themselves." ~W.C. Fields.

Rule #4: Follow the Money (Capital)

At one time the United States was the best place to invest and do business. More wealth was being created here than anywhere else in the world. When Warren Buffett began his career, stocks were cheap, Americans saved, and we were exporting products all around the world. Things have changed.

We need to adjust our frame of mind and start looking outside our borders for investment growth and wealth preservation.

Developing economies look just like ours did back in the early 1900s. It would be foolish not to invest in some of these other markets. China, Brazil, Asia and India will be great places to invest for a long time precisely because they're emerging markets.

Billions of people are just now discovering the joys of free markets. The entrepreneurial spirit is beginning to kick in on a global scale. A great deal of creativity, drive and innovation will outpace even our rosy growth expectations for these regions.

I remember reading an article recently about how surprised investment analysts were that Singapore's GDP rose by 38%. We'll continue to see such surprises.

"Concentrate your energies, your thoughts and your capital. The wise man puts all his eggs in one basket and watches the basket." Andrew Carnegie.

What Forbes Magazine Tells Us

The economic explosion that's occurring in Asia and around the world can clearly be seen by flipping through Forbes magazine's list of the 400 richest people in the world.

When I read through the 2010 issue and looked at the statistics, I fully grasped the reality of globalization for the first time.

These are some of the telling facts you should be aware of:

- *For the first time*, the richest man in the world is from a developing country (Carlos Slim Helu of Mexico).
- The number of Chinese billionaires *doubled* last year—despite a worldwide economic depression.
- The number of billionaires in 11 other developing countries also *doubled* last year.

- There are now 89 billionaires in China—the 2nd highest number behind the U.S.
- The number of billionaires in Asia grew by an astounding 80%! Of the 403 billionaires on the Forbes list, 234 reside in the Asia-Pacific region.
- Only 16% of the 97 new billionaires on the Forbes list are from the United States.
- The increase in wealth isn't restricted to just the super wealthy. According to the Merrill Lynch-Capgemini World Wealth Report, Asian millionaires are, for the first time, wealthier than their European counterparts.

Commitment is the ignitor of momentum. ~Peg Wood.

Why Capital Is Important

All this growth in Asian economies has an unseen, yet to be realized effect.

First, driven people in *developed* countries such as the U.S. are being attracted to these emerging markets for work. We're seeing Chinese immigrants return home for better opportunities. The Chinese have a name for them: "The Returning Turtles."

We should expect this to continue for various reasons. This "gold rush" mentality to get a piece of the action will result in a brain drain from U.S. and European economies. We must not underestimate the vital importance of the movement of capital to Asia.

Money and intellectual capital, two of the most important causes of prosperity, always rush to where opportunity exists, where wealth is being created. Entrepreneurs are always attracted to predictable and profitable opportunities. And in the age of information, relocating is very easy.

America's *greatest* asset, the one thing that's helped it grow *more than anything else,* has been its national *prosperity consciousness.* America has always been seen by the world as *the* land of opportunity. That ideology has driven ambitious entrepreneurs to our shores for decades and reinforced that initial belief. It's been a self-fulfilling prophecy. China has created this same prosperity consciousness. The average man on the street believes that this is their century. *China Inc., has become a spiritual brand.*

What we must realize is that the *effects* of this movement of human capital, spiritual optimism and money will intensify wealth accumulation in the

East. This should tell us where and how we should invest our money if we'd like it to grow.

"Optimism is the faith that leads to achievement. Nothing can be done without hope and confidence." ~Helen Keller.

Everyone Who Has It Will Have More

There's a Bible passage that illustrates my point: "For to everyone who has will more be given, and he will have an abundance. But from the one who has not, even what he has will be taken away." Capital works like that. If you've got it, you'll get more. If ya ain't got it, you'll lose what you've got left.

In May 2010, for example, more capital investment flowed into China than in any other month on record. That same month, their exports rose 50% from the previous year despite the European debt crisis and a major recession in the United States. Think about the significance of a 50% rise in exports for the largest exporter in the world. The growth is a result of capital accumulation in China.

When capital accumulates in a given economy, it's like coil springs tightening up which will soon uncoil and release all of its pent up energy. As capital flows to Asian economies, growth will intensify in the coming years. The boom will continue. It may have its hiccups but it will grow dramatically.

Any hiccups their economies experience will be from the irrational fear that what happens in Squirrelmerica and Europe affects Asia. It's not true. Investors are beginning to see that Asia can stand on its own. We've finally seen proof of something called "decoupling"—the West is no longer necessary to maintain global economic growth.

The flow of capital is just another reason we can expect Asia to grow at a rapid pace. To put that growth in perspective, China is the largest car market and the second largest market for Rolls Royce—a luxury car company that sells its models at a price tag of $400,000.

"He who gathers money little by little makes it grow." ~Proverbs 13:11.

Business and Professional Strategies

So how does a small business owner, investor or a professional take advantage of this huge growth trend? The most obvious way to take advantage of the growth is to simply start a business in one of these booming economies. Relocating might not be the easiest way to do it, but it's probably the most profitable.

A more passive way to take advantage of the growth is to place the bulk of our money in dividend paying companies located in some these developing economies. We can also invest in developed economies like Japan, Australia, South Korea and New Zealand that will gain tremendously by supplying China with finished goods or natural resources.

> *"Debt, n. An ingenious substitute for the chain and whip of the slave driver."*
> ~Ambrose Bierce (The Devil's Dictionary, 1911).

Rule #5: Follow the Leaders

To make good investment decisions, you must follow people who've been good predictors in the past. Some of the people I follow (Warren Buffett, Jim Rogers, Marc Faber and Peter Schiff) have made great predictions in the past and I'm sure they'll make great ones in the future.

If they're good predictors, they're great entrepreneurs in the true sense of the word. An entrepreneur not only makes good predictions but also puts her money where her mouth is. That's the difference between entrepreneurs and nutconomists—one group risks capital whereas the second doesn't.

Entrepreneurs always know more about their industry than economists do. As a general rule, Kidus, you want to follow successful entrepreneurs (forecasters) and rely less on economists in building your business. We've got other reasons not to rely on economists' predictions then that they're inherently less reliable than entrepreneurs.

As I was listening to a lecture by economist Murray Rothbard, I found out that economists in the professional forecasting business call each other up to check their forecasts with each other! Apparently, when their economic forecasts are wrong, they have a great excuse: "Well, don't blame me. I predicted the same thing all the other leading economists did."

In other words, they collude with one another; don't be fooled by experts or authorities when you get here. Their collusion may explain why so many of them failed to see the scale and scope of the current economic crisis. This just goes to show that we're all in the thick jungle of global commerce with machetes in hand—we must clear our own paths.

We can be knowledgeable with other men's knowledge, but we cannot be wise with other men's wisdom. ~Michel de Montaigne.

Rule #6: Follow the Central Bank

Let's face, predicting the future ain't easy. But we still do it. And as long as someone in the marketplace is making more money than everyone else, we know they're doing a better job of guessing.

What I'm about to tell you will help you become a much better guesser. This will give you a huge competitive advantage by giving you a better crystal ball. If I were to ask you what one thing makes educated guessing hard, you probably wouldn't say a central bank unless you've taken the time to study the banking system in depth.

But that's just it. Our central bank, Federal Reserve, (we'll call it the Fed for short from here on) makes the entrepreneur's job much more difficult than it has to be. Every investor must understand how the Fed affects their ability to make money.

"It is well enough that people of the nation do not understand our banking and monetary system, for if they did, I believe there would be a revolution before tomorrow morning."
~Henry Ford.

Is You Rich or Not?

As you read the following description, keep this in mind: When we make something for our customers, we must know whether they'll have the money to buy our products or services. This isn't brain science. It's how the world works (Gold Diggers don't look for sugar daddies in the ghetto). Here's how it works for real estate entrepreneurs.

When the Fed arbitrarily lowers interest rates (borrowing costs) to 1%, demand will go up and prices rise because more people *seem* to be able to afford more stuff. If interest rates go *up*, demand will *fall* because the cost of borrowing is higher.

Here's the problem: We have no idea *when* the Fed will screw up our plans. They can make your customers become poor one day and rich another by giving them a line of credit or by taking it away. This continual, arbitrary adjustment of interest rates makes the entrepreneur's job more difficult than it has to be.

"A bank is a place where they lend you an umbrella in fair weather and ask for it back when it begins to rain." ~Robert Frost.

The Problem With Real Estate

Do you ever wonder why all across the globe, real estate developers seem to be super rich one day and bankrupt the next? Why don't we see the ketchup industry going through boom and bust cycles?

Real estate developers and investors have gone bankrupt, lost their fortunes, their homes, and marriages because of *false entrepreneurial calculation.* When rates are *artificially* low, these entrepreneurs are fooled into thinking home buyers have more money than they do.

Because buyers feel richer than they are, demand for housing goes up. Buyers tell real estate entrepreneurs, "I got mad cash. Build me my dream home!" The real estate entrepreneur then starts building more expensive, longer term, capital intensive projects because buyers have got all this new credit. As the credit gets spent, it pushes everyone into higher income brackets. Wages go up when credit floods the economy and buyers can show higher earnings on their W-2s to qualify for bigger loans.

Everyone's saying, "Forget the Spam and canned Tuna baby, I want me some caviar and exotic fish I ain't even heard of before!"

For the real estate developer demand is demand. They see the go signal and they go for it. They don't have time to study monetary policy and understand the ins and outs of how the Fed operates. He just wants to do his job and make some money.

"The more the government 'plans', the more difficult planning becomes for the individual."
~Friedrich Von Hayek.

The Big No-No

So the entrepreneur mistakes *credit* for *wealth*, and *debt* for *income*. He invests his money and time to build the million dollar homes.

All his predictions are based on one, really big *illusion*. People can't really afford what he's planning to build, but he thinks his project will be profitable based on current economic conditions. He doesn't understand that his customers ain't got real money (savings) to afford what he'll make.

In fact, buyers couldn't even afford the new plasma TVs and nutsoline guzzling NUTS-UVs they've purchased. Instead of saving and investing, people are borrowing to consume.

Developers have two *seemingly* rational reasons for being optimistic. First, they expect that credit will be available for their customers (homebuyers). Second, everyone's real pay looks like it's increasing. They are overly optimistic about the future because money is flowing.

So developers take the cue: They start building lots of homes. So now, both consumers *and* producers (i.e., homebuyers and developers) are actually *dependent* on continued credit expansion. The credit being pumped into the economy to stimulate growth is creating an addiction to credit caused by irresponsible spending (which was encouraged in the first place by the Fed).

"Rather go to bed without dinner than to rise in debt." ~Benjamin Franklin.

The Central Dealer

When the Fed starts raising interest rates to calm the fake boom they've created, even less people can afford to buy the developer's finished product than before the boom began. The availability of too much credit always causes people to foolishly spend their savings. What real estate investors eventually find out is that, not only have potential customers spent all their *real* money, but they're in more debt than ever before. Fewer people can afford to buy million dollar homes without credit (debt).

Look at the horrible timing of the Fed. They raise rates *after* everyone has spent their real money (savings) and need credit the most. It's as if we have a Central Drug Dealer handing out free drugs on every street corner, turning people into addicts and then suddenly outlaws drugs.

This is a snapshot of how the Fed creates boom and bust cycles. *You must understand where you are in relation to this cycle.* When the central bank lowers the rate of interest to stimulate the economy, understand that the following *boom* is simply a mirage, a hoax. Don't take the bait. When credit is cheap, save more, when credit isn't available buy discounted assets.

"From now on, depressions will be scientifically created." ~Charles Lindbergh Sr.

Rule #7: Experiment

Kidus, I cannot do enough to stress the importance of experimenting in building your money making skills. Experience is the greatest teacher of all.

Experience helps us make sense of the information we get from books, it also increases its usefulness. The more we experience, the more we'll learn how the world of money runs; we'll be able to connect the dots and trace wealth effects to their causes.

When Napoleon was giving advice to military officers, he told them that, "tactics can be learned from books but knowledge of the higher aspects of war can be acquired only through experience, through the study of the history of wars and of the battles of the great captains. Can we learn how to compose a book of the *Iliad* through the study of grammar?"

Obviously, we can't become great poets simply by studying grammar. But that's what most people do in life—they simply study *the grammar of prosperity*. We must therefore, compose, draft and rewrite our business plans in order to become successful. But above all, we must not fear failure—we must *act*. After all, can we learn to make money by simply studying business?

"All life is an experiment. The more experiments you make the better." ~Emerson.

Recap: Seven Rules for Entrepreneurial Life

The seven rules I've presented are ways to make sure your bet—be it a business venture, investment or a job—is a good one. In order to become successful nutpreneurs, we must (1) Learn from History; (2) Master Luck; (3) Find the Right Environment; (4) Follow the Money; (5) Follow the Leaders; (6) Follow the Central Bank; (7) Experiment.

These are all methods of reducing error (i.e., guaranteeing success)—the whole point of nutpreneurship, investing and meaningful work. These rules are designed to make the nut accumulation phase a lot easier and far less risky. If you read this letter a second time, you'll notice that at every turn, I've pointed out ways to reduce your risk while increasing the likelihood of financial gain.

Wealthy people don't gamble with their money. Neither should we if we wish to join their ranks.

Your Loving Uncle,
 Akinaw.

Part II

*The Secrets of
Economic Literacy*

Why You Need
Economic Literacy

Dear Kidus,

We have a saying in the U.S. that goes, "You're only as strong as your weakest link."

When it comes to building wealth, our weakest link can literally make us or break us. Fortunately, there are only four links in the wealth building chain—entrepreneurship, economic literacy, capital management and productivity. Not understanding these four principles is the cause of most financial failures and economic recessions.

For example, as critical as entrepreneurship is in building wealth, that skill alone isn't always enough to keep and grow the wealth you've created. After all, whether you hold on to your profits as cash, invest in bonds, treasuries, real estate, stocks, or simply choose to spend it, *something* must be done with what you've earned. You must make a decision.

Know this: Every decision has a financial consequence. Regardless of what you invest in, your decision will add to or subtract from your net worth.

Crossing the Hidden Line

I hinted at this need for economic literacy when I gave the example of a good entrepreneur who made $100 million but ended up losing $96 million when he entered the real estate business. That entrepreneur's name is John McAfee, founder of McAfee Incorporated—the virus software company. You can see his name in red, bold type on hundreds of thousands of pages online.

So, why did a seasoned entrepreneur lose so much money? It staggers the mind. There's no doubt that he's a great entrepreneur, no one can argue that. Years before the technology boom, he was an experienced computer programmer. He must have had great entrepreneurial sense to see the market potential of computers in the 1960s. It must have also taken a great deal of courage to quit a day job and start a business in the computer virus industry.

So what happened? What caused McAfee to lose $96 million if he was such a talented entrepreneur?

The answer is simple: McAfee, like 95% of the world's population, didn't understand *true* economics. He might've learned a bit of it in college, but he most likely didn't learn the correct theory of economics—the only true theory of economics; it's not taught in our school system (you'll find out why).

Economic literacy would have told McAfee that when he ventured from the software business to the real estate business, he was crossing a big line. The software industry is in the consumer goods industry while real estate is in the capital goods industry.

Although crossing that line is such a big deal, most real estate investors don't understand this basic point. During the last eight years, I've had thousands of discussions with real estate investors but I don't remember one about the special risks of working in the capital goods industry.

Everyone just believed real estate prices would never go down. So why did real estate prices collapse? We've already answered this question (Rule #6).

Each market sector has its special risks but the real estate industry is more likely to go through boom and bust cycles because property prices depend on interest rates, not just supply and demand.

The real estate crash which started in 2007 is really the result of Alan Squirrelspan's policy of keeping interest rates too low for too long. As he started to raise rates to avoid inflation, millions of people who had bought *into* the bubble he created were about to see their dreams burst.

That's what Squirrelspan did—in the hope of temporarily stimulating the nutconomy he baited millions of squirrels into buying overvalued tree houses. Home builders were also baited into building an oversupply of homes because they mistook false, inflationary demand for real demand.

What McAfee didn't realize was that real estate feels the abuse of the Fed's arbitrary power to change interest rates (the cost of debt) more than other industries. It does so because property values are denominated in *debt*.

Consumer goods industries like retail and food, don't experience huge boom and bust cycles. That's why we never see a boom or bust cycle in the ketchup, chicken, mustard, hamburger or mayonnaise industries. Those things must be bought with cash.

People don't buy properties with cash; they buy it with debt (this means most homeowners can't afford their homes!). Property prices go up and down with the cost of debt like a thermometer does with the temperature of a room.

I don't think McAfee understood this difference.

"An educated person is one who has learned that information almost always turns out to be at best incomplete and very often false, misleading, fictitious, mendacious—just dead wrong."
~Russell Baker.

The Economics of Fried Chicken

A lack of economic education affects our financial lives in other ways. Of the possible illustrations that can be given of the importance of economic literacy, one of the best is a story about one of the most recognizable faces in the world.

The story of Colonel Sanders and the Kentucky Fried Chicken restaurants he created is both uplifting and a bit sad. It's uplifting because he never gave up on himself or his dreams, the mark of a true entrepreneur. For years, he worked odd jobs from steamboat driver to a railroad worker. He kept striving.

While he was taking odd jobs, he was also taking correspondence courses to become a lawyer. That career ended after he reportedly got into a fist fight with a client in the courtroom. Then he owned and operated a gas station which also served as his home for awhile.

But as the saying goes, "You can't keep a good man down." Instead of giving up, Colonel Sanders remained open to the possibility of success. And guess what? Opportunity knocked.

Sanders began serving meals out the back of his gas station. Meal after meal, he kept searching for the right recipe for his fried chicken. While he was looking for that perfect recipe, he started gaining popularity and more people came to taste it (I'm getting hungry thinking about it). To keep up with demand, he built a restaurant that could seat up to 142 people.

Two years later a fire burned down the restaurant—but not his dreams. The Colonel built another restaurant, and added a motel to it this time. He opened the door, started the fryer, rooms filled up, seats filled up and so did his bank account. But then…another tragedy struck.

A new interstate highway was built that drastically reduced traffic to his restaurant. When most people would've quit, Sanders refused to give up on his dream. He auctioned off the restaurant and motel, took his now famous secret chicken recipe and hit the road in the hopes of selling franchises.

It worked. He was about 65 years old when he began to strike it rich by franchising Kentucky Fried Chicken restaurants. It took him a long time to build up his entrepreneurial skill but he had done it—a great story of never giving up. The story gets really interesting when we look at what happened after he achieved that initial success. While looking at his fascinating story, I learned that Sanders didn't really understand the stock market or finance. You see this fact come out in the way he decided to sell his company.

When Colonel Sanders sold KFC to a couple of investors, he sold the brand for a measly $2 million. It was worth way more than that. The investors who purchased the business from Sanders turned around and sold the business for $275 million just *7 years later!* There's more to the story.

Along with the $2 million purchase price, the investors offered Sanders 10,000 shares in the new company, but he turned it down because he didn't understand what was being offered to him. As a result, Sanders' net worth was barely a nickel more than the secretaries who took stock options in the company before it went public.

Sanders had, through years of ups and downs, become a great nutpreneur and built a regional brand, which would soon become the biggest restaurant chain in Squirrelmerica but failed to add financial education to his skill set. Here's the point of this story.

Without understanding how to value an asset, you're always in danger of making a bad trade, purchase or sale. Not knowing how to value things is the one thing that can negatively affect all your nutconomic activities.

Most people will have an opportunity to be able to sell or trade whatever asset they own for a profit or a loss. *When* we sell and *how* we sell depends on how we judge value. In order to understand how to value assets, you must become economically literate. The two investors who initially purchased KFC made the better trade because they understood the intrinsic value of the business they were buying. So did the KFC workers who traded pay for stock.

"The roots of education are bitter, but the fruit is sweet." ~Aristotle.

Going for Gold

Knowing how to avoid a possible financial catastrophe (McAfee) and knowing when and how to sell an asset (Sanders) are two big benefits of economic literacy. These are very practical skills to build because we'll have to use them at some point. After all, most people will own a home or own shares in some kind of a business or have an investment portfolio.

One other benefit of economic education is being able to make bold business or investment decisions. Henry David Thoreau once advised us all to,

48

"go forth boldly in the direction of [our] dreams, live the life [we've] imagined." Becoming wealthy requires that we become bold. But boldness requires something else.

In order to be bold, go all out, or "put the pedal to the metal" or "put a little boogie in it" or "put a little wet on your whistle" or "get jiggy with it" or "put your back into it" or…sorry, I'm getting carried away. To go all out, we must first understand what we're doing. We must figure out how the system works; we must understand our economic *context*.

If you've observed parents who have a few young children in the same age range, you've probably seen a glassy, dazed look in their eyes and a face painted with touch of desperation. I get that look whenever I go shopping with my fiancé. I don't know where I came from or where I'm going. I'm thirsty, hungry, cold, confused and tired. I've got a look of hurried confusion.

You can see that same look on the faces of people standing in unemployment lines. Millions of people have this feeling of complete disorientation, not knowing what will happen next or why things have happened. It's a horrible feeling—especially when it comes to money, business or investing.

About a year ago, I remember talking to a business owner who began to cry in the middle of our meeting because she didn't know why business slowed so much, why costs were increasing and when things would turn around. She didn't feel like she was in control. She had no context.

Without context, there's no meaning and in the absence of meaning, anxiety always fills the void. Being able to understand our economic system gives us a sense of control and the peace of mind that we're doing the right thing with our money.

Realizing big dreams requires big courage. You can't go for gold without nutconomic education.

"With confidence, you have won before you have started." ~Marcus Garvey.

My Lack of Economic Literacy

When I first decided to become a career entrepreneur, around the age of 19, I was reading Forbes and other financial publications from cover to cover.

I started working with Primerica Financial Services, the marketing branch of Citigroup. By the time I was 23, I was enrolled in an MBA program with an emphasis in financial services.

I quit my MBA program a third way through for spiritual reasons and instead, finished a Master's degree in a program not directly related to business.

Throughout my educational odyssey, I experimented with different business ideas. I didn't fully embrace any of them except for real estate. After receiving my M.A., I went into the real estate business full time and did fairly well for a number of years until the crash was under way in late 2007.

It wasn't until this crisis that I realized I'd been floating along on incomplete economic ideas even though I'd been learning financial concepts since I was a teenager.

I understood what financial commentators were saying in articles, but now realize, I didn't fully understand why they were saying it. Professionals in the real estate and financial industries just operated on widely held assumptions because they're salespeople. They don't get paid to accurately know how much things are worth. They're not there to educate investors.

"A hallucination is a fact, not an error; what is erroneous is a judgment based upon it."
~Bertrand Russell.

Where's the North Star?

We didn't know that we didn't know because there were no *competing* economic ideas. We didn't have a way to "judge the economic judgers" so to speak. It looked as if economists made *random* predictions from the same murky pool of economic theory.

At least in the court of law, legal judgments are based on something higher and above the court itself, to which any citizen can appeal in self defense. In the U.S., the Constitution and prior court decisions are appealed to as the ultimate basis of judgment.

If something is *unconstitutional*, no amount of maneuvering or complicated legal arguments could make it *constitutional*.

Making a good financial decision depends on something *higher* than finances, just as a legal decision depends on a higher legal code or a Constitution. I understood financial principles and terminology better than most people but I didn't get that *financial* literacy was useless without something else—*economic* literacy.

Economic literacy helps us know if our financial decisions are wise or not. Economic literacy is to financial decisions what a rudder is to a ship or the North Star was to the old navigators. It tells us if we should trust the proclamation of financial priests. When it came to financial matters, most people didn't have a way to check the soundness of ideas they'd heard on television or in print.

All around the world, masses of people grovel at the altar of the high priests of finance situated in government or banking positions, taking it for granted that they've really heard the voice of God, that they're speaking *the* economic truth and that they have the people's interest in mind.

I saw something in the real estate crash—a clue that showed me something wasn't right if only very few economists were able to predict what was to happen. Our omnipotent Federal Reserve with its staff of 400 plus economists didn't see the collapse coming. Why?

How could so many professional forecasters and analysts fail to predict a recession of this magnitude? Why didn't I see this impending doom? To be fair, some economists were predicting a recession but only a handful (literally) predicted an economic catastrophe.

"Get your facts first, then you can distort them as you please" ~Mark Twain.

The Priest Have No Robes

The only conclusion I could come up with at first was that most economists are wrong most of the time.

In fact, if you listened to what most economists *were* advising, even after the financial meltdown was under way, you'd be in a bad position today.

Even after the economic crisis was *under way*, I remember hearing economist Ben Stein (among others on a CNBC panel), tell viewers that financial companies like Bear Stearns and Merrill Lynch (which were about to go broke), looked like good buys! Unbelievably, he's out with a new book called *"Bulletproof Investing."*

When you get to the U.S. Kidus, remember that the "economic priests have no robes." They have no real credit although they're back in the limelight as if nothing happened. Most economists belong to a school of economics called "Keynesianism", an ideology that's partly to blame for America's massive debt. *Before the housing bust, economists from this school were telling us that if Americans owned their own homes, they didn't need a retirement account!*

They preached the ridiculous idea that a home was a good *investment*, when it's really a luxury. They also believe that higher asset prices means there's more real wealth in the economy. By that logic, Zimbabweans are the richest people on earth since it takes $500 billion to buy a loaf of bread.

They say other crazy things like "deficits don't matter." But as the legendary investor, Marc Faber pointed out in a recent presentation to the Mises Institute, one of these Keynesian economists said deficits don't matter a week before the Greek _debt_ _crisis_.

You don't need intermediaries, priests and oracles; what you need to do is go directly to the Source yourself. That Source is a system of sound economic ideas—a deep pool of wisdom—from which you can draw out and apply sound financial principles by the bucketful.

This Source is your "think tank" that'll guide your entrepreneurial life. And, remember that there's no other way to build a prosperous life than by being an entrepreneur in some capacity.

I'll introduce you to this Source in our next letter.

Your Loving Uncle,
    Akinaw.

The Few Economists
You Can Trust

Dear Kidus,

Bill Cosby once said something that's helped people accept the fact that they're getting old: "When you become senile, you won't know it." There's some consolation in that.

But there's no consolation in not knowing your own economic environment and how it works. You'll be conscious of the fact you don't know what you're doing when you lose money. In this letter, I will introduce you to a group of economists that know what they're doing. Their ideas have been tested; they've repeatedly been found to be right about almost everything.

The Few, the Proud, the Austrians

So, how do I know that the economic ideas you're about to learn are not theories but *the* truth. Well, if we revisit what we learned in 7th grade science class about the scientific method, we know that a hypothesis is only true if it has the power to *predict*.

If a scientist makes a statement that's contradicted by experience, then we know that it's false. In the same way, if an economist makes a false prediction, his economic *theory* is false.

My principles of wealth creation are partly based on a theory that's best predicted economic events accurately from the Great Depression of the 1930s to the current Alan Squirrelspan recession.

Economists of this school are kind of like the nerds of the economics profession. They're unpopular but they're always right. You want to sit next to them in class. They're unpopular because they're truthful and non-ideological. Nutconomists usually sell their souls and brain power to one of two ideologies: a warfare state or a welfare state.

Being an Austrian economist is, in my opinion, almost professional suicide because it's completely non-ideological—exactly why we should listen to them. Not surprisingly, many people haven't heard of them.

What's called "Austrian" economics is really the only true science of economics. If you want to understand economics, study their works. *This*

53

knowledge alone will save you a lifetime of confusion and financial heartache. It's called *Austrian* economics because the founder of the school, Carl Menger, was an Austrian.

Once again, I know this theory is true because their predictions are always correct. *And if you want to be a good entrepreneur, if you want to make money and hedge your bets carefully, you must listen to what they've got to say.* Their ideas will make the road to riches much less risky. If you read their works, you'll have a whole new world opened up to you; you'll feel as if you'd just woken from a long nutconomic dream.

And, as I've shown, what most Squirrelmericans think they know about nutconomics is merely propaganda because various organizations have an *interest* in our ignorance. It should, for example, be obvious that we can never stimulate an economy through spending because the money for the stimulus must, *of necessity*, come from the very economy we're trying to stimulate.

Below is a summary of the most important and practical ideas these honest economists have contributed.

"An honest answer is the sign of true friendship." ~Proverbs 24:26.

Two Economists

Two Austrian economists, Ron Paul and Peter Schiff, have recently gained some notoriety for being able to predict the current crisis in detail. I'll introduce you to this school of economics through the views of these two men.

"Wall Street is the only place that people ride to in a Rolls Royce to get advice from those who take the subway." ~Warren Buffett.

The Alien Congressman

One of the *few* politicians who truly understands how the economy works is one of my heroes—Congressman Ron Paul.

I admire him because he's a weirdo. I mean, not only is he an incredibly honest politician, he also has a first rate economic mind. You'd see he 'gets intellectual with it' if you get to know the brainiac behind the public veneer. If you hear him speak, you'd recognize he doesn't have a lying bone in his body and he always appeals to the best in us. Honesty goes a long way with me because I realize that most professional economists, squirreliticians, political

54

commentators and presidential advisers simply lie and appeal to the worst part of us to get ahead.

He's never taken a bribe or a government loan, he didn't allow his children to take out student loans, and he's one of only two public officials not participating in the lucrative Congressional pension program. He even gives part of his salary back to the Treasury every year. He also wants to preserve the wealth of younger generations—right down my alley.

As an investor, I'm really interested in what he's got to say because he's always right about the future. And unlike other Austrian economists, he's understandable to the average squirrel.

His uncanny predictions are one of the reasons I call him the alien congressman. He's either an alien or, just happens to know the right economic recipe. We can learn quite a bit about his economic method by looking at his predictions.

"Honesty is the cornerstone of all success, without which confidence and ability to perform shall cease to exist." ~Mary Kay Ash.

2008 Crash

His most recent prediction was made during the 2007 presidential primaries when he warned we were on the brink of economic collapse—something he's been warning about since 2003. No one listened. After all, people don't enjoy facing the reality of impending doom. Denial is always a stronger motive than realism.

Paul's predictions were fascinating for two reasons. First, he didn't have anything to gain personally from what he was saying. Second, I noticed during the course of my research, that he's predicted another crash years before it occurred.

"All this worldy wisdom was once the unamiable heresy of some wise man." ~Thoreau.

1987 Crash

If you go on Youtube.com, you can see that Paul even predicted the stock market crash of 1987 during a debate with a Federal Reserve Bank governor in 1983.

Maybe the more surprising thing about that debate was that a congressional official knew enough about the economy to publicly debate an economist. Most politicians don't even understand basic economics.

"Common sense in an uncommon degree is what the world calls wisdom."
~Samuel Coleridge.

Fannie Mae/Freddie Mac

Back in 2003, Paul also predicted that Fannie Mae and Freddie Mac (our government backed mortgage providers) would help create a mess in the mortgage market. He said that by guaranteeing mortgages, the government is attracting more money into the housing market, thereby making the bubble even bigger.

In other words, government was encouraging over-investment in housing. Congress, according to Paul, was adding fuel to the fire:

"Ironically, by transferring the risk of a widespread mortgage default, the government increases the likelihood of a painful crash in the housing market. This is because the special privileges of Fannie, Freddie, and HLBB have distorted the housing market by allowing them to attract capital they could not attract under pure market conditions. As a result, capital is diverted from its most productive use into housing. This reduces the efficacy of the entire market and thus reduces the standard of living of all Americans.

However, despite the long-term damage to the economy inflicted by the government's interference in the housing market, the government's policies of diverting capital to other uses creates a short-term boom in housing. Like all artificially-created bubbles, the boom in housing prices cannot last forever. When housing prices fall, homeowners will experience difficulty as their equity is wiped out. Furthermore, the holders of the mortgage debt will also have a loss. These losses will be greater than they would have otherwise been had government policy not actively encouraged over-investment in housing." ~Ron Paul Sept. 10, 2003.

"The man of knowledge must be able not only to love his enemies but also to hate his friends."
~Friedrich Nietzsche.

Housing Bubble

As you can see in the 2003 address above, Paul was one of the first to predict that there *was* a housing bubble underway when hardly anyone else saw it. What's more remarkable is that he doesn't say that the real estate crash wouldn't occur if the government hadn't created programs to subsidize housing. He's merely saying the *inevitable* losses "will be *greater than they would have been* had government policy not actively encouraged over-investment in housing."

In other words, he knew that 1) there was a bubble, 2) it had more than one cause, and 3) one of them was Fannie and Freddie. I've not heard another politician ever make such a *subtle* differentiation of economic facts.

"The difference between stupid and intelligent people—and this is true whether or not they are well-educated—is that intelligent people can handle subtlety." ~Neal Stephenson.

Iraq War

Paul's economic education has also helped him predict the outcome of events not even related to the economy.

In the run up to the Iraq war, for example, Paul predicted it would be longer and more costly than what was being projected. He said Iraqi tribal disputes would make governance unmanageable and that more troops would be needed to secure Iraq than what officials were suggesting.

Others said it would be quick, we'd be welcomed as liberators, we had all the troops we'd need, and oil revenues would pay for the cost of the War.

We now know that Paul was right. We say that hindsight is 20/20 but for this strange Congressman, *foresight* seems to be 20/20. How did he know all these things? What economic ideas gave Paul the ability to predict the future outcomes of all these *different* events?

"Never was so much false arithmetic employed on any subject as that which has been employed to persuade nations that it is in their interests to go to war." ~Thomas Jefferson.

Decline of the Dollar

Paul also predicted the deterioration of the dollar's value. And he's been right about this too. From 2002 until 2010, the dollar has lost about 35% of its purchasing power (its value). That means that the total value of our savings, nutchecks, homes, stocks and everything else, has also declined by 35%.

This government created dollar devaluation is one of the biggest reasons people should be investing in foreign companies that earn money in *appreciating* currencies.

"A dollar saved is a quarter earned." ~John Ciardi.

Peter Schiff's Predictions

A lot of Peter Schiff's predictions are similar to Paul's in substance but wider in scope. Interestingly, just like Paul, his predictions were made *years* before people even began to get that there was a problem.

Schiff predicted the real estate crash, the wider recession, the financial collapse, the decline of the dollar, the rise of commodity prices such as gold and oil, the strength of commodity rich nations such as Canada, New Zealand and Australia, as well as the depth and even the length of the Squirrelspan Recession. Both Paul and Schiff were laughed at for their predictions.

"Business more than any other occupation, is a continual dealing with the future; it is a continual calculation, an instinctive exercise in foresight." ~Henry Luce.

Why Predictions Matter: The Cash Value

Predictions are lifelong silent partners that help us avoid mistakes and ensure we reach our goals. Men have certain instincts that they've genetically received that help them avoid doing some things because they can predict negative consequences.

One of these instinctual rules was summed up by Tim Allen: "Never comment on a woman's rear end. Never use the words "large" or "size" with "rear end." Never. Avoid the area altogether. Trust me."

Unfortunately, we don't have an economic instinct that helps us choose our financial actions carefully. It has to be learned. But there is a big promise for taking the time to accurately learn from Austrian economists. The biggest benefit, in my view, is being able to avoid making disastrous financial decisions.

But on the positive side, the cash value of their ideas is this: If you can predict where the market will be, you're on your way to building real, lasting wealth. You've found the only "money making system" that exists. If you know

Google's stock will go up 100%, well then, you should buy it. If you know Google's stock will be going down, you can also make money by betting against it. The important thing is to know where the stock is going. If you can predict market ups and downs, you're set.

During the housing crisis, the people who saw the crisis coming and bet against sub-prime mortgage lenders or bank stocks, reaped huge, unheard of profits. I remember getting a call from someone in the real estate business as the crisis was underway who was telling me that his bosses were, "Making a sick amount of money—getting rich—by betting against these mortgage banks."

How much money can be made from betting against stocks? Hedge fund manager John Paulson received the *largest one year payout in Wall Street history* of $4 billion by betting against subprime mortgage companies. It pays to be able to predict the future—it pays to be a good entrepreneur.

The examples above just show some of the many ways to make money with economic literacy. Now, obviously, the money John Paulson made may never be made again so quickly. But on a smaller scale, Paul and Schiff have done quite well by betting on the future of gold prices and other commodities.

"Nine-tenths of wisdom is being wise in time." ~Theodore Roosevelt.

Why Prediction Matters: Professional Strategies

Real estate used to be a glamorous business. There was a ton of money to be made in it for investors and workers alike. If you had a real estate job from 2001 to 2006, people would've thought you had great timing although we were really in the middle of a fake boom. Loan brokers and agents were easily pulling down six figure incomes. But what if you stayed in the business for another two years?

You would've realized you made a big mistake by getting into the business in the first place. From 2001 to 2006 the real estate industry created millions of jobs *on credit*. So not only would you have lost your job (which was inevitable as credit dried up) but you would've also lost five years of experience in a field of work you should have been in the first place. When the thousands of workers that should never have been in the real estate industry look for other work, they find out that they're less competitive.

We don't always understand the full costs of the Fed's power to alter an economy's structure. But it can cost you dearly. One of the negative side effects is that it momentarily diverts human capital from where it can best serve society. This is why predictions matter to the wage worker just as much as it does to the investor. Economic education is _not_ just for business owners.

"The only place opportunity cannot be found is in a closed-minded person." ~Bo Bennett.

Zero Growth or 400% Return

During his 2007 presidential campaign, Paul had to disclose some of the publicly traded stocks he owned. Turns out, he was heavily invested in gold, silver and other metal mining stocks. What do you think the cash-value of Paul's recipe was?

If you look at the graph below, you can see the price of gold has almost _doubled_ since 2007, when Paul publicly released his holdings. Of course, since I now get his brand of economics, I'm positive Paul owned gold, gold related or other precious metal mining stocks years before 2007. Look at the chart below again. If you knew what Paul knew in 2001, your return on gold would have been 400%! Again, the key word is _if_; a lot of people didn't know what he did.

As a side note, this upward rise in gold prices may just be the beginning. Gold miners are digging deeper and faster than ever before but are unable to keep up with global demand. Obviously, Paul made a very good bet— *the return on gold has been better than almost every other asset class over the last 10 years.*

"The general who wins the battle makes many calculations in his temple before the battle is fought. The general who loses makes but few calculations beforehand." ~Sun Tzu.

The Lost Decade

Other people who didn't understand economics weren't so lucky.

Everyone else who invested in real estate or the stock market didn't see *any* gains from 2000 to 2010. Imagine 10 years of zero growth! We now refer to the last 10 years as the "lost decade."

What makes the lost decade sad is that people had plans that they can't go through with now. Some wanted to retire, start a business, go to college, get married or travel. All these plans had to be set aside because of one thing: They didn't understand economics.

Most people can't afford to lose another decade. After all, we only get 8 of them to start with—maybe 9 if you're rich. By the way, referring to the last 10 years (2000-2010) as the "lost decade" is quite optimistic because it wasn't just a decade of zero growth but of *negative* growth.

Although the net worth and incomes of Squirrelmericans have not gone up during the last 10 years, nut prices have. If you account for inflation, they've lost more like 15 years. No baby boomer can afford another 15 years of zero growth.

People are ready to educate themselves about money after experiencing what Time magazine has called the "decade from hell." How long can people stand to take the abuse of Keynesian or political nutconomists? I predict there'll be a huge wave of squirrels looking to empower themselves in the areas of finance and nutconomics in the years to come.

I see this trend in my students. One day, I explained how money, banking, government debt and the Fed work together. The lecture ended after identifying the various causes of our economic crisis and its significance for their careers. During a break one student asked me, "Based on what you said in class, are you more of an independent or Libertarian now?"

"Well, I think those are the only two choices we've got—especially for younger people who will inherit the massive debt they've created", I replied.

"Me too", she said, "I'm definitely more of an independent nowadays and I think a lot of people are leaning that way because they finally see how Washington works."

We can't blame people for seeing the government as the problem—especially with the enormous amount of debt it's created, not to mention playing a big role in the economic crisis. Most people's 401(k)s are now 201(k)s.

I wonder what their financial lives would look like if, like Paul, they knew enough to buy gold a decade ago or if they'd known that our government was creating a housing bubble in 2003, five years before the resulting financial collapse. They'd be 400% richer today.

That's the value of what you're learning. In our next letter, I'll show you why the Austrian economists are always right.

Your Loving Uncle,
    Akinaw.

How to Understand Your Financial Universe

Dear Kidus,

We can learn a lot from comedians. They just have a way of summing up our most complex life situations into simple statements.

Tim Allen, for example, has a clear grasp of sociology: "Women now have choices. They can be married, not married, have a job, not have a job, be married with children, unmarried with children. Men have the same choice we've always had: work, or prison." What more needs to be said?

As I now explain why Austrian economists are right about the future, keep in mind that it's all actually very simple.

How Did They Know it?

So, what gave Ron Paul and Peter Schiff (and other Austrian economists) such clear economic foresight? How does one economic school predict every recession of the last hundred years?

It turns out, their powers of insight are based on common sense ideas that are available to the rest of us but only if we look just a little bit below the surface and get rid of some basic economic and political assumptions that we've been trained to accept as fact.

"All over the place, from the popular culture to the propaganda system, there is constant pressure to make people feel that they are helpless, that the only role they can have is to ratify decisions and to consume." ~Noam Chomsky.

Principle #1: It All Starts with a Precise Definition of Money

To understand the American economic system, you must get a clear, precise grasp of money, credit, and inflation. We should start with money anyway since our net worth is denominated in paper currency.

Two things determine the value of our money: 1) The supply of dollars (arbitrarily determined by the Fed), and 2) the strength of the economy.

Paul has a nagging suspicion that government will *always* do one thing to our money—it'll increase the supply of money to pay for its expenses. But that causes the dollar to be worth less.

Here's how it works: As the government keeps printing money, the additional dollars they add into the system dilutes the purchasing power of the ones already in circulation. And since Congress will keep printing money to handle its deficits, *Paul predicts that the dollar will lose value over the long term.*

We also have history as a guide. Whenever the Fed has increased the supply of money (we'll get into this later), it's never taken that extra liquidity back out of the system. In other words, the printing will never stop. And this continual expansion of the money supply has another effect.

The price of everything in the economy rises because it takes more dollars to buy the same amount of stuff. Government printing of money is the *only* reason *all* prices go up year after year. *It's the only thing that causes system-wide inflation.* Because Paul understands this process, he knows that holding his wealth in paper dollars is a major liability.

He doesn't invest in U.S. Treasury notes or bonds or CDs because he knows inflation will eat up his wealth. Real inflation, according to trustworthy economists is anywhere between 6 and 9% even though our government says it's historically been between 3 and 5%.

The government, by the way, doesn't factor in all costs in measuring inflation. For example, it fails to accurately represent housing cost increases in its measurement. But why would they? The lower inflation *looks*, the more money they can justify printing.

Paul is aware of all these games, dishonest statistics and figures. Because he expects the government to continue to make each dollar worth less by printing trillions to pay for its expenses, Paul puts his money in gold and other things that the government can't print.

Investing in gold is a *defensive* move based on an understanding of what governments *always* do to the supply of money. What you know has consequences. If you want to avoid the pain of financial loss, you must understand how money works.

"Paper money has had the effect in your state that it will ever have, to ruin commerce, oppress the honest, and open the door to every species of fraud and injustice."
~George Washington, (letter to J. Bowen of Rhode Island, 1787).

Connect the Dots

From that initial fact that government printing of money will reduce the value of each dollar, you can draw *other* conclusions. You can answer a large number of investment questions based on a correct understanding of money.

"Paper money eventually returns to its intrinsic value—zero." ~Voltaire

What About Domestic Stocks?

Investing in American stocks that earn income in *dollars* runs into the same problem because the value of dollar denominated dividend payments will be reduced by the rate of inflation. Imagine that you invest in an American company paying a 6% dividend. If you're being paid in dollars that are losing 7% of their value every year, your *real* dividend payment is a negative 1%. Various financial advisors still preach that the U.S. is a good place to invest but we must recognize it for what it is: propaganda.

"Do not buy the hype from Wall St. and the press that stocks always go up." ~Jim Rogers.

Inflation Adjusted Nation

The Fed's misrepresentation of inflation numbers is the biggest problem with inflation adjusted investments like annuities or treasuries. You may still see a negative return despite the supposed adjustment. If inflation is 7% but your adjustment is 3%, you're losing 4% on your investment.

But a negative return isn't all you've got to worry about. For the first time in our history, there's a real chance the dollar might collapse.

I used to think that was an alarmist position. How could the dollar collapse? But once you understand the history of paper money, you see it's possible because every nation that's had paper money has experienced a currency crisis or runaway inflation (Germany, Argentina and most recently, Zimbabwe are a few, famous examples).

"A prudent question is one-half of wisdom." ~Francis Bacon.

No Money, No Problem

Ron Paul decided to run for office *because* he understood money. He got the political bug when President Nixon decided to completely get rid of something called the "gold standard" in 1971. America had been under some form of a gold standard since its founding.

Under the gold standard, every dollar the government printed had to be backed by a certain amount of gold. That meant paper money was kind of valuable—it wasn't monopoly money yet and since there was a limited amount of gold to back each dollar, there was a limit on spending. This was a major inconvenience for our government. They wanted to spend more but their credit card had a limit.

Before Nixon got rid of the gold standard, when other countries wanted to redeem their dollars, we would pay them in gold. But the U.S. was running out of money (real money—gold). In order to continue the War in Vietnam and around the world, as well as pay for the War on Poverty, the War on Drugs, and other major expenses, Congress needed money.

So, Nixon decided to increase the government's credit line by refusing to pay for expenses with real money (gold). After his decision, our money was backed by paper and ink. If we had debts, we paid with paper and ink.

When Paul saw what we had done, he saw it for what it was—the U.S. was declaring *bankruptcy*. We had no more gold (real money) to pay for our debts. But we had plenty of debt to pay for debt. *Debt had become money.* But Paul also saw something else: He must've known we'd take on so much debt that the value of the dollar could one day collapse.

"Inflation is when you pay fifteen dollars for the ten-dollar haircut you used to get for five dollars when you had hair." ~Sam Ewing

Principle #2: Money, Government and Human Nature

George Carlin once summed up a man's fear of commitment: "'I am' is reportedly the shortest sentence in the English language. Could it be that 'I do' is the longest sentence?"

Like most fears, it's really an irrational one. Married men are actually very happy as long as they do what they're told. But there is a commitment that every Squirrelmerican should fear—marriage to endless debt. This marriage is an unholy union of government and paper money.

The wealth of the nation through the abandonment of the gold standard has been placed in the hands of a few secretive and unethical bureaucrats. Credit is the most addictive drug humanity has ever experienced. If government is allowed to print as much money as it wants, it'll always want to print just a little bit more.

Year after year, one administration after another, politicians are always increasing something called the debt ceiling. It was originally intended to keep the national debt from rising above a certain maximum limit.

Calling it a debt ceiling is amusing. We should just call it a debt *floor* because the ceiling of a previous administration becomes the floor of the next.

Why does debt keep increasing? Both political parties under Nixon, Carter, Reagan, Clinton, Bush and now Obama, have raised the debt ceiling.

Why can't they stop the compulsive spending? They do it because they can. They do it because voters don't know enough about economics to end the Federal Reserve System. The Fed is the entity through which the government secretly steals nuts from future generations of squirrels.

Politicians use the printing press to make promises to the people who vote for them—to pay for votes without seeming to raise taxes. And in this way, they *institutionalize* debt. It's an illusion of course; all spending is paid for somehow. That somehow is called the inflation tax. Americans don't like taxes but they like to spend the wealth of future generations on either social services or war.

Based on what we know of the American political and economic system, we should expect that the value of the dollar will eventually collapse.

Rating agencies have been threatening to downgrade our government's credit rating but no politician has been paying attention (except Paul of course).

When the U.S. does lose its undeserved top credit rating, there'll be a big price to pay as the cost of borrowing increases dramatically. In the next five years, according to current estimates (without factoring in a lower credit rating) the annual cost of interest payment on government debt could reach $1 trillion! American taxpayers currently pay $400 to $500 billion per year of *interest* on debt.

These are just some of the reasons I'm advising my closest friends and family members not to own any stocks or bonds of U.S. based companies or hold onto cash. After all, history has shown that societies don't change unless they go through some kind of a major crisis, and even if they do go through such a crisis, they end up making worse choices in response to it. Nazi Germany and the Soviet Union, for example, were irrational responses to economic crisis.

If you remember in my letter on entrepreneurship, I told you that a good entrepreneur needs to have a sense of the "flow of history". Paul has a good grasp of the rise and fall of empires. All empires crumble when their currencies do. We have no reason to believe that our dollar's value will not crumble.

> *"We learn from experience that men never learn anything from experience."*
> ~George Bernard Shaw.

Principle #3: Bubbles and Busts

Predicting the decline of the dollar's value may seem simple enough. After all, if you dilute anything, that thing becomes less valuable. We only value scarce things.

That's simple to understand. However, when we come to the subject of economic booms and busts, we think it's harder to get. Despite what we may think, if Schiff and Paul were able to foresee these booms and busts, we should be able to do as well.

But first, let's remember why this is important: In investing and in business, timing is everything. We know, for example, that recessions are times when there's an enormous transfer of wealth from sellers to buyers. We also know that in economic booms there's a huge transfer of wealth from buyers to sellers. When you buy in a bubble, you're drastically overpaying—losing wealth and hard earned money. When you sell in a bubble, you're reaping a huge profit.

Many people have heard the motto that an investor should "buy when there's blood on the street" (referring to Wall Street). But how do you know when the street is about to bleed? You obviously need to know in order to save up cash to take advantage of the situation when it arises. If you don't know, you may find yourself bleeding *with* the Street.

So how come Paul, Schiff, Marc Faber and other Austrian economists never seem to be bleeding with the Street? Why do they usually end up unscathed? Alan Greenspan once said that we can't know if we're in a bubble, but those guys always seem to know.

Paul was warning Greenspan about the formation of a real estate bubble way back in 2003! *Does this mean Paul knows more about the nutconomy than our exalted Alan Squirrelspan? The thing that's so strange about this scenario is that Paul knew more about the consequences of Greenspan's actions—the very person in charge of managing the economy!*

Austrian economists know that one of the best ways to find out if you're in a bubble is to keep an eye on what our government is doing to the *supply* of money in the economy. When the central bank pumps too much money into the economy by lowering rates (as Alan Squirrelspan did for years after 2001), asset prices (real estate, bonds, stocks, etc) rise dramatically and a bubble is created; but when the Fed takes the money back out of the economy to avoid inflation, the bubble bursts.

Austrian economists didn't take the bait when asset prices rose dramatically as a result of Greenspan's irresponsible credit expansion—they knew the boom was a hoax. Booms and busts are almost always a result of too much credit.

The Great Depression of 1930s, for example, was a result of flooding the economy with too much credit during the 1920s. In his book, *America's Great Depression*, economist Murray Rothbard, points out that bank credit expansion increased by over 68% from 1921 to 1929. In those same pre-depression years (1921 to 1929), bank lending to stock speculators rose 750%! Think about the incredible amount of risk people took without knowing they were doing so.

Investors were (a) *borrowing* money to (b) buy *inflated* stocks which were soaring because of (c) the *initial* credit expansion created by the Fed. Some speculators may have known they were playing Russian roulette but they didn't know the gun was fully loaded.

"Getting rid of a delusion makes us wiser than getting hold of a truth." ~Ludwig Borne.

Principle #4: Economic Growth

These two economists also have a clear and precise idea of economic growth. Sustainable economic growth comes from saving and investment rather than borrowing and spending. You need to know this in order to make wise business decisions. When do you load up on inventory? Should you hold on to your assets? You would if you expect the economy to grow. Should you scale back your expenses because you expect the market to cool?

If you listen to mainstream economists, their answer to combat recessions is to expand credit (debt). But Austrian economists argue that increasing the amount of debt in our economy just kicks the can down the road, creates a bigger bubble and leads to greater consumption of capital. It doesn't increase production and jobs.

Providing the economy with too much credit (debt) increases the trade deficit because it encourages Squirrelmericans to buy more imported nuts. Debt isn't the solution, it's the problem. What the U.S. economy needs is less credit, less spending, more savings, more investment, more production and more exports.

Understanding the causes of economic growth is one of the most important prerequisites to becoming a successful investor. With that understanding, we can choose the right economic environment to grow our investments.

Beginning with the country first, allows us to make more money safely—regardless of the investment class you choose. It's the starting point. Economies comprised of savers and producers do better than borrowers and consumers. This is the reason why unemployment has been decreasing for 13 straight months in Germany. It's an export driven economy, Germans don't over consume.

"By continually pushing the message that we have the right to gratification now, consumerism at its most expansive encouraged a demand for fulfillment that could not so easily be contained by products." ~Ellen Willis.

Principle #5: Interventionism and Unintended Consequences

Austrian economists also base their predictions on the idea that government intervention anywhere—in the marketplace or in foreign affairs—always produces a bigger problem than what it seeks to address.

We need to understand this concept in order to avoid being *consequenced* by government actions. Government actions have big, *unintended consequences* that directly affect our financial lives. For example, in order to "stimulate the economy" after 9/11, Alan Greenspan began flooding the economy with credit by lowering interest rates to 1%. In December 2001, the rate was 1.82%. Two years later in December of 2004, the rate was finally lifted to 2%.

In 2006, the rate was still a very low 5%. The economy was literally *awash* with money because Easy Al kept rates absurdly low for five years in the hope of stimulating the economy. As a result, we experienced one of the biggest bubbles in American history.

"We shall not grow wiser before we learn that much that we have done was very foolish."
~Friedrich Von Hayek.

It's the Stupid, Stupid

Now let me explain how stupid we'd have to be to think we can stimulate an economy by expanding credit. First of all, the public mistakenly thinks that government bureaucrats are smart when the truth is that they're shortsighted, unethical and arrogant. Here's Greenspan's reasoning...

Step one: He thinks flooding the economy with money will stimulate growth. But there's just one problem with that plan: *The Fed can't control what people do with the money once they get it.* Think about how logically absurd it is to expect to stimulate the economy by printing money *without* controlling *how* and *where* the extra money is spent! That means the Fed tries to stimulate the economy with the admission they can't control the *outcome* of their actions! Read this paragraph again slowly and you'll get why the Fed should *not* attempt to regulate the economy.

Here's how Easy Al's plans went awry: Instead of taking the stimulus money to expand our economy by producing exportable goods, the public used the money to buy massive amounts of imported goods, thereby weakening our economy even further. We didn't build new factories, roads, or manufacturing plants—we just spent an enormous amount of money. As Peter Schiff has pointed out in his book, *Crash Proof,* Greenspan initiated the largest consumption binge in American history.

Greenspan should've realized this. After all, we've dismantled our industrial base and shipped manufacturing jobs to Asia. Almost everything is made in China, Germany or Japan. We're a nation of consumers. Instead of stimulating our economy, the credit expansion stimulated the economies of Asian exporters. The graph below tells the story:

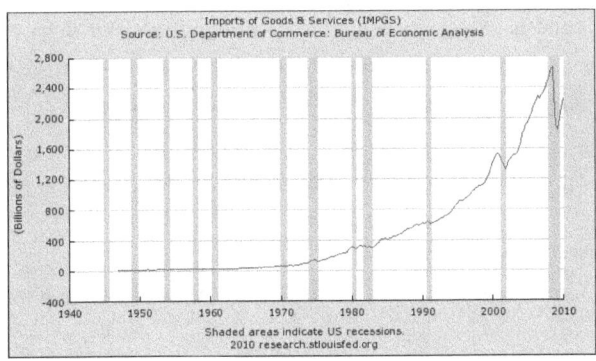

71

Look at the sharp rise in imports from 2001 to 2007. In that time of easy credit, imports more than doubled from $1.3 trillion to $2.7 trillion. *The one thing you don't do when our industrial base has been dismantled is give people money!*

The effect of all this spending on imports meant only one thing: Jobs for exporters—not for us. Asian economies have been able to build up their industrial base with *our* money thanks to Easy Al. The huge transfer of wealth from the U.S. to Asian economies was just one of several "unintended consequences" of too much credit. Government policies sometimes create the very situation they seek to avoid. These bureacrats aren't gods. As I've shown, Ron Paul was warning Alan Greenspan of the consequences of his actions. How scary is it to realize Squirrelspan was making *decisions* for our economy although he couldn't *see the consequences of his own actions*? It's as scary as realizing he doesn't understand why stimulating the economy is logically absurd.

> *"All the perplexities, confusion and distress in America arise, not from defects in their Constitution or Confederation, not from want of honor or virtue, so much as from the downright ignorance of the nature of coin, credit and circulation."* ~John Adams.

Recession and Credit Contraction are the Cure

We must understand something else about the above graph. If you look at it again, you'll see that spending on imports only decreases during recessions (the shaded areas).

When the Fed increases credit, our economy suffers because money and therefore, jobs flow overseas. In other words, our economy only improves when easy credit is not available to finance imported goods. Economic depressions are the cure, not the problem. Politicians will *never* tell the public that what we need is a deeper recession to quickly fix all of our problems. Their only motive is to create the *illusion* of prosperity to get re-elected. Our economy needs to deleverage, we need to get rid of the excess credit.

> *"If borrowing and spending all this money led to more jobs, then we would be at full employment already."* ~Paul Ryan.

Unintended Consequence: The $500 Billion Tax No One Knows About

There's another unintended consequence of the Fed's easy credit policies. The following graph shows oil prices for the last 5 years.

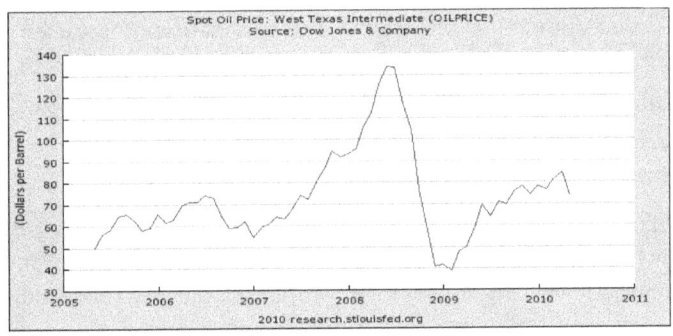

The strange thing about this graph is that when oil prices started to rise dramatically in 2007, we had *just entered into a worldwide recession*. At its peak in 2008, prices reached $140. This jump in price is strange because *no one pays more for a commodity they expect to be used less*. Doing that would be like paying double for bread that's about to go stale.

Why would oil prices skyrocket when the demand for oil was decreasing due to a worldwide recession? That doesn't make any sense. Well, it does make sense when you realize interest rates were dropped significantly late 2007 and into 2008 after the recession was underway. Take a look at what interest rates did as oil prices were rising dramatically.

The shaded area in the graph below shows the large drops in rates occurred at the same time the price of oil went up (shown in the graph above). In the second half of 2007 and early 2008, investors had access to a lot more credit as rates dropped. All the extra credit created speculative buying and just like real estate, oil formed a bubble of its own.

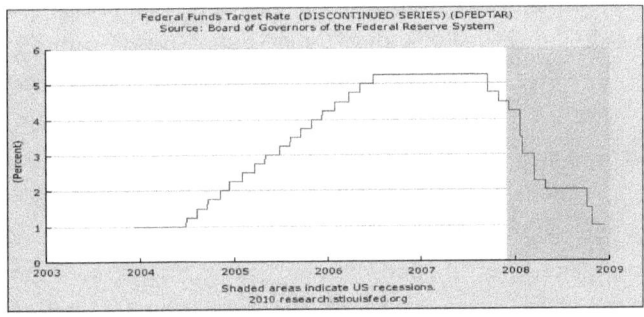

As the price of oil skyrocketed, so did the cost of gasoline. Squirrelmericans spent an extra $500 billion on oil during that period of credit induced speculative buying. That $500 billion cost was only incurred because the Fed flooded the market with credit. The speculation it produced resulted in a tax on the consumer—an *unintended* tax—but a tax nonetheless.

Kidus, if you were here when gas prices rose to over $4/gallon virtually overnight, you would've seen quite a spectacle. A lot of people were really angry, but they directed their anger at oil companies instead of looking at our Fed's monetary policy. Presidential candidates were priceless with all their posturing and idiotic solutions. They'd stop to fill up gas for photo ops, called for a "gas tax holiday" and oil windfall profits tax but not one candidate could diagnose the problem. We now know why prices rose so fast.

> *"The government solution to a problem is usually as bad as the problem."*
> ~Milton Friedman.

Foreign Policy

This idea that government actions have *unintended consequences* applies to foreign policy as it does to the economy. And our foreign policy has a *huge* effect on our pocketbooks. It's not only America's *biggest* expense (bigger than Medicare or Social Security) but it affects our livelihoods in other ways.

Paul's understanding of interventionism explains why his predictions are accurate even in matters unrelated to the economy. But neither his foreign policy predictions nor the logic behind them should surprise us.

Something some Americans know in their hearts to be true but may not want to admit is that terrorism is, in fact, a response to our intervention in the affairs of foreign nations. I had a hard time admitting this fact myself. But all we must do to understand why Arabs hate American foreign policy is look at what we've done to them throughout the 20th century. No one with an open mind can look at the history of the region and fail to understand they have a reason to be angry.

Terrorist acts are predictable because terrorism is the only response Arabs have to American aggression. Arab states have been, until recently, run by brutal, puppet dictators that have (for the most part) been installed in power by the United States. Unified opposition to American aggression was impossible for Arab citizens. The response of terrorism is what the CIA calls "blowback." It means that our aggression/intervention in the affairs of other nations has unintended consequences.

It's politically incorrect to say these things but as I mentioned, Americans already know this to be true in their hearts. Why else would the 500 plus page publication of the 9/11 Commission Report *fail to mention the causes of terrorism just once?* Not *once*?

Why would the commission leave out the most important part of the investigation? Is there a more important question to ask than, "What causes terrorism?" The cause of terrorism was never identified by the commission because they knew the answer. Any psychologist will tell you that truth isn't to be found in what *is* said but what's *not* said. The commission report's true findings can be seen not from what they've included in their report but from what they've *systematically omitted*. They must think we're stupid enough to believe the 'official' findings.

The 9/11 Commission Report committed one of the biggest Freudian slips in American history. It says in big, bold type: "Our foreign policy is to blame. *We* messed up. *We* did something wrong."

Terrorism isn't about religion. After all, the Pope lives in Italy. There are more Christians in Brazil and in Europe than in the United States. France, of all places, has gone much further than the U.S. ever will by actually outlawing Muslim women from wearing Burkas (face veils).

And terrorists don't hate us for our freedom. Here's a short list of other free nations: Austria, Canada, Mexico, Britain, France, Germany, Australia, New Zealand, Costa Rica, Brazil, South Africa, India and the list goes on (you get the point). For some reason, none of these other nations are called the "Great Satan" by terrorists.

What's important to note is how our foreign policy affects our pocketbooks. We've paid dearly for our interventions across the world. I only mention all this because we don't learn about this in Business 101. But we live in a large interconnected world, it must be looked at.

"Bad taste is simply saying the truth before it should be said." ~Mel Brooks.

Round and Round We Go

Speaking of interconnectedness, here's a sequenced order of unfortunate events that illustrates this idea of the unintended consequences of government action:

1. Our government intervened in the internal affairs of Arab states (installing hated dictators like the Shah of Iran, Saddam Hussein, etc.).
2. These events together caused the Sept 11th attacks.

3. We then had to intervene in the economy. After Sept 11ᵗʰ 2001, Alan Squirrelspan attempted to stimulate it by increasing credit.
4. And because Easy Al kept rates too low for too long, a real estate bubble formed and burst.
5. And because the real estate bubble burst, current Fed Chairman Ben Squirrelnanke dropped rates to the floor.
6. And because he lowered rates, oil speculators bid up the price of oil which then created a $500 billion tax on our economy. And round and round we go.

If the government had done nothing, we wouldn't have experienced the Sept 11ᵗʰ attacks or the current economic recession. Is there a more powerful case for not allowing government to make important decisions? Its bad choices affect everyone else in the system because government *collectivizes* failure. We pay for its failures. Every American paid for *Alan Greenspan's* failures because our economic actions are collectivized through the power of the Federal Reserve.

In conclusion, this non-interventionist philosophy is a big reason (maybe the only reason) the Austrian theory of economics is unpopular, although it has a sterling reputation for making accurate market predictions, something that can make you rich.

Interventionism is popular around the world because as human beings, we're fearful. We want to neutralize *perceived* threats. When we hold an image of a threat in our minds, we forget it's only imaginary. We try to neutralize imaginary threats and create *real* ones in the process.

"Don't be afraid to see what you see." ~Ronald Reagan.

The Blessing of Acceptance

I used to wonder why it's so difficult for us Squirrelmericans to understand how things really worked. But I now know why: Pretending not to know is a powerful temptation.

The *misrepresentation of common sense* in economics, politics and foreign policy is precisely what's wrong with the American system and why it'll destroy itself *if* it doesn't learn to accept reality.

We can pretend not to know the truth but there's just one problem with that: Our lives don't matter—we die knowing we were just a cog in the machine. Fitting in has never brought anyone feelings of pride and accomplishment. I once heard someone say that "If there's a hell, it must be a state of being consciously aware of having lived a conventional life of no consequence."

Inconsequential people don't think—they do what they're told and believe what they're told to believe. I feel like I was saved from living a life of no consequence, because I would've been just an unseen blip in human history if it wasn't for the hand of Providence. I was plucked out of the remotest part of the earth—I was given a chance. I wake up every day knowing that I could've been a poor, uneducated, shoeless farmer in the outskirts of Ethiopia.

In my view, America's magnificent inheritance is a chance at being free from delusion and ignorance. Others aren't so lucky. Millions of people in North Korea wake up every day to worship a little tyrant. Some Americans wake up to worship their own tyrants—fear and cherished superstitions. But unlike our North Korean friends, we don't have to. We have a chance to live in truth if we choose to do so. The only tyrant we ought to have is our conscience. Ghandi put it best: "The only tyrant I accept in this world is the 'still small voice'."

My feeling is that millions of people can identify with Pinocchio when he said, "I want to be a real boy." People are tired of the lies, misrepresentations and confusion that plague their minds. Well, in order to be a real boy or girl, to grow up, to have a mind of our own, we must start admitting the possibility we can be wrong. I've done it, it's doesn't hurt as much as you may think. There are big financial consequences of failing to accept reality as it is.

"Our intention creates our reality." ~Dr. Wayne Dyer.

We Know What We Know

We can all intuitively understand economics. In fact, we know a lot more than we think we do. Intuition is what gives mothers the ability to know when their kid's lying. They can get past dad with something a little better than, "The cat peed on my broccoli", even if you don't have a cat. But the crap stops with mom. She just knows.

This internal way of knowing is the only thing that fear can't exploit. It's an immediate awareness of things as they are. Christians can relate to this idea in the following way. When the Apostle Paul wrote, "You have the mind of Christ" and then added, "Therefore, *you do not need a teacher*", he was saying that believers have *immediate* access to truth without an intermediary. He was saying there's no barrier between man and God.

In ancient Israel, there was a barrier between God and man. If Jews wanted access to God, they had to go through a priest. But Paul was saying the priests are now out of business. There are no gatekeepers.

I'm saying the same thing about economics. The priests have failed and our foreign policy has also failed. It's time to fire the economic priests. The experts have secretly run the economy and our foreign policy for 100 years— and they've messed it up in ways *they* don't even understand. They then repeat certain phrases until we believe it (i.e., "credit is the lifeblood of the economy"). We don't need to listen to them. They have no credibility.

If we can add and subtract, we can understand economics—like Pinocchio, we can be a real person. All the graphs, charts, studies and different types of economic schools just show us that economists have a hard time grasping or accepting reality.

In any case, I'll close by saying that non-interventionism is the biggest barrier and obstacle of accepting the only true theory of economics—Austrian economics. Don't be a statistic. It's why most people haven't heard of this school of economics. Truth doesn't appeal to fear. Cowards always want more control, more force, more guns, less freedom, more wars and higher taxes.

All our problems stem from cowardice, not tyranny.

"An economist is a man who states the obvious in terms of the incomprehensible."
~Alfred A. Knopf.

Conclusion

We conclude, then, that without economic literacy, we cannot make responsible financial decisions.

We can see that there can't really be different schools of economics for much the same reason that we don't have different schools of adding. True economic literacy can only be learned by studying the so called "Austrian school of economics". You can start by reading Henry Hazlitt's, *Economics in One Lesson.*

I've shown some of the reasons why they're able to predict future economic events so well. You can use these same principles to predict future events. Remember, based on 100 years of evidence, as long as the government does *anything*, we can predict it will mess that thing up. Knowing this one fact can help us profit by betting against what government does or at least, we can avoid its consequences. And if you haven't noticed, it's easy to do Austrian economics because one idea leads to another. It is causal, connective and rational:

1. For example, since the U.S. government has the ability to print money without taxpayer consent, *then* it will print too much.
2. If it prints too much, *then* the national debt will continue to rise and the value of the dollar will fall.
3. If the value of the dollar falls, *then* prices will continue to increase.
4. If the government pumps too much money into the economy to "stimulate it" *then* an asset bubble will form.
5. If an asset bubble forms, then we'll have a bust.

In closing this letter, I'll quote one of my favorite writers, C.S. Lewis. He once said that, "…if we admit God, must we admit a miracle? Indeed, indeed, you have no security against it. That is the bargain."

In the same spirit, I'd like to add the following: "If we admit government intervention, must we admit economic demise? Indeed, indeed we have no security against it. That is the bargain."

There are *no* surprises.

Your Loving Uncle,
    Akinaw.

Making Money With
Economic Literacy

Dear Kidus,

By now, you may realize economic literacy isn't hard to master if we can find the courage to put aside assumptions and prejudices.

Even if we don't want to become economists ourselves or manage our own money, we can at the very least, judge the credibility of financial advisers we may want to hire. Living with the financial confusion that plagues billions of people around the world is a choice.

My intention in this letter is to sharpen your economic mind a bit more before moving on to capital management—the third principle in the money making process. We'll look at practical examples of what's happening right now in the global marketplace and see how we can take advantage of it.

You'll learn there's a process to investing profitably in the marketplace. Many people who are struggling in this economic environment want financial freedom but may not know how to create it. Unfortunately, a lot of financial books and commentators tell us what needs to be done but fail to show how to do it. They hardly ever encourage in-depth economic thinking based on good assumptions.

Rich Dad Mania

One of the most popular financial books of all time is *Rich Dad/Poor Dad*. It has sold more than 25 million copies to date.

The author's main point is that people need to accumulate assets instead of liabilities. Assets put money in your pocket while liabilities take money out. On that basis, he showed that a home isn't an investment because it takes money out of your pocket. To be rich, you need to buy assets and get rid of liabilities. The book's main value is that it accurately shows Squirrelmericans why their financial lives suck.

Although I enjoyed the book, I felt it was incomplete. It didn't teach people when and how to accumulate assets. It also made the asset accumulation process look easier than it is. Accumulating nuts takes focus, courage, *accurate nutconomic knowledge* and energy.

81

More importantly, people need economic education more than they need financial education because financial decisions depend on economic reasoning. In other words, you must be able to interpret the handwriting on the wall—not just know that something's been written.

Kiyosaki made a wonderful case for financial literacy, but a better case can be made for economic literacy. We must go a little deeper.

"Ask and it will be given to you; seek and you will find; knock and the door will be opened to you." ~Matthew 7:7.

Our Dogmatic Slumber

In any event, it feels like Americans have woken up from a very long sleep. We feel much the same way philosopher Immanuel Kant did when he famously said that he awoke from his "dogmatic slumber" by reading the writings of David Hume. We're also waking up from our dogmatic slumber by reading the economic facts that confront us.

Our biggest assumptions are being tested. Maybe spending doesn't stimulate the economy. Maybe printing money won't bring us economic salvation. We're finding out we have a lot of catching up to do in educating ourselves. It's only then that we can make things right in our financial lives.

When I was in seminary, my roommate had left the TV on one Sunday afternoon. A local preacher in the Los Angeles area was talking about people who have chaotic lives.

"Chaotic people don't have chaotic lives", he said.

I said to myself, "I thought that was the point of the sermon?"

He continued, "Chaotic people have chaotic *minds*. If we don't have order in our minds, in here [pointing to his head] we can't have order out there in our physical world. In order to have the life that you want, you must have the mind that can produce that life."

In a similar fashion, the Western world has created a very chaotic economic climate because our thinking has become clouded. We must clear up the fog 100 years of bad economic thinking has imprinted on our collective consciousness.

We've got confused states of minds because we see profit in self delusion. I believe every man on the street knows the grave economic danger of allowing our government to run the printing press but he secretly wishes it to continue in the hope of increasing his own credit line. We've seen the fruits of bad economic thinking—it's time to start over.

"'Tis this desire of bending all things to our purposes which turns them into confusion and is the chief source of every error in our lives." ~Sarah Fielding.

The Logic of Investing

We can find a great deal of clarity about how to think about investing by using an analogy from the world of physics. If we understood just one law of physics and applied it to our investing decisions, we would start building wealth at a much faster rate because we'd be able to make responsible choices with our money. At the very least, we would be able to avoid disastrous financial mistakes.

The law of physics I'm referring to is Sir Isaac Newton's idea that every action has an equal and opposite reaction. Married men understand this law very well. They know the equal and opposite reaction of forgetting to leave the toilet lid in the down position.

Here's how it applies to thinking about money. Whenever you make a financial decision that you do see (you take an action), you automatically make another decision that you don't see (reaction). When you spend all your money today, you're also choosing not to invest in a lucrative business idea that could come your way tomorrow.

One of the most common expressions you hear from people who have missed out on a great opportunity is, "But I didn't have the money to invest at the time." That's not exactly true. A more accurate statement is this: "I spent the money I could've used to invest on other things like alcohol and parties."

Just because you can't instantly see the consequences of your financial decisions doesn't mean they don't exist. When you think about the *effect* today's financial decisions have on your life tomorrow, you're thinking like a good economist.

If Newton was an investor, that's how he would've looked at money: "Think Isaac, think....what's the equal and opposite reaction of what I'm about to do with my money right now?"

When he looked at the world of physical motion, he said something so simple and so obvious that it's a surprise you can become famous for doing so. Does it really take a genius to see that if something happens, something else must've happened first?

Can making a good investment be that easy? Can understanding the economy and the financial markets be that simple? Yes. If you can understand cause and effect, you're on your way to a lifetime of financial prosperity. That's the art of economic thinking.

It's a lot like the discipline of mathematics. It wasn't until college that I learned *why* I was learning math. Math just helps us learn how to think. Every answer to an equation is actually given in the problem. One side of an equation must equal the other.

As the economist, Henry Hazlitt said in his great little book, *Economics in One Lesson*, the art of economic thinking is not just looking at the immediate but also the longer term *effects* of any act or policy. Economic thinking is involved in *tracing the consequences of our actions*.

Another way to put it is that for every Ying, there's a Yang. This is the sum of economics. If you have too many Yings per Yang, then a problem will result. It's a matter of ratios (this is why government policy is very useful in predicting future outcomes—government action always messes up the ratio by adding to many Yings to Yangs).

When I first read Hazlitt's book, I had the feeling that things were finally "adding up". I had a deep knowing that what I was reading was true.

"Against logic there is no armour like ignorance." ~Laurence J. Peter.

Learning to Trace

So how do we use the art of economic thinking to our benefit? It's really a matter of tracing consequences.

Every day, money can be made by simply looking at the longer term, secondary, unseen effects of the market's decisions. To illustrate how this works, I've first listed some economic facts we do see and have then traced secondary consequences we may not see.

1. *China's currency is undervalued.* What's the secondary effect?

If China's currency is currently under-valued, then we can expect it to rise at some point. If China's currency rises by 5-10% in the coming year, any investment in the Chinese economy would return at least that much even if there was no real growth in price of the underlying stock.

We can take this line of reasoning one step further.

If the currency appreciates 5 to 10% in the next 12 months, then a super smart thing to do is buy Chinese companies that pay dividends. The logic for doing so is that the dividends (paid in the Chinese Yuan—its currency) will also appreciate. If we earn dividends in the Yuan, we can, therefore, add another 5 to 10% to the equity growth in our stocks. Pretty simple right?

Well, why stop with China's currency? What about the dollar? The value of the dollar has dropped 35% over the last seven years or so. This means that any dividends paid in dollars will depreciate. That 35% deprecation is just the market's opinion of the value of the dollar. Remember that inflation is also eating away 6 to 9% of the value of dollar denominated dividend payouts.

2. *Chinese Worker Salaries are increasing.* What's the secondary effect?

As hundreds of millions of Chinese workers start getting paid more for their labor, their domestic consumption will increase because they'll have more money to spend. China, then, will be able to buy more stuff from the rest of the world. But as Chinese consumers begin to spend more, Squirrelmericans will no longer have the advantage of having cheap Chinese exports subsidize their standard of living.

One way to take advantage of this fact is to invest in Chinese companies that are ready to feed growing domestic demand. Find out what Chinese citizens have a taste for that they can't yet afford. Luxury goods makers with the most exposure to the Chinese market are good bets. If there's anything I know about the *New Rich*, it's that they want to enjoy the things they once couldn't afford.

As China's domestic demand grows, their imports will also expand. The price of natural resources and energy will also rise as hundreds of millions of people start to consume much more than they are now. China is already the largest consumer of energy.

3. *U.S. States, the Federal Government and Municipalities are raising hundreds of billions of new capital by selling more bonds to pay for their debts.* What's the effect?

First it means that our debt ridden state and federal administrations are competing with businesses and citizens for loans. That, in turn, means that the price of loans for Squirrelmericans will be more expensive.

There's only a limited amount of capital in the marketplace. Our government is *competing* with its citizens to get its hands on that credit.

If the government was *not* in marketplace competing for loans, the supply of available credit would increase and loan costs for businesses and individuals would go down. An increased supply of funds and a lower number of borrowers will lower costs.

The irony is that you hear city, state and federal officials call for more credit for the private sector even while they make the credit problem worse. *This is a real, unseen tax on the private sector.*

Generally, the American public doesn't realize the massive amount of taxes they pay because they don't see all the different ways in which they do so. Higher loan rates are just one example. But there are other ways. Our standard of living is also taxed when government competes with businesses for loans because capital will be diverted from more productive uses in order to pay interest on government debt. We'll have less to invest in other things like better food, better roads, medical cures and better education as a result.

4.   *The U.S. government is continually running huge deficits.* What's the effect?

Based on this fact, I can predict first that by 2013, the U.S. government will lose its AAA credit rating. After that happens, the cost of borrowing money will increase.

As the rest of the world becomes less dependent on the U.S. economy, and sees other safer places to invest, capital will flee to foreign markets, thereby aggravating the credit problem even further.

In order to fund its debts, the government will print a massive amount of money and increase taxes significantly. This printing of trillions of dollars, in turn, will lead to massive inflation and civil unrest (we're already seeing this).

As this happens, the government will come up with new, ingenious ways of raising money (through some form of taxation)—but it won't reduce its size or expenditures, it's looking for unconventional ways to raise taxes. The U.S. is the only industrialized nation that taxes the incomes of citizens living abroad. Citizens living abroad will be forced to give up their citizenship to avoid this double taxation (Google "Time.com Expat" to see a Time Magazine article about this fact). We'll see more people renounce their citizenship as a result.

I also predict our government will make it very difficult, if not impossible to move money abroad. Remember that inflation is the government's secret weapon in paying for its expenses. It's a secret way of confiscating the wealth of its citizens without their knowledge. But confiscating private wealth is difficult to do if money flees Squirrelmerica's borders—money must remain within our borders in order to be taxed.

This is a major reason why people (baby boomers especially) need to invest in foreign stocks. If people are thinking of retiring comfortably overseas, now's the time to do it. They shouldn't wait for inflation to devalue the dollar and make living abroad more expensive. We'd be losing in two ways by waiting: Foreign currencies will be rising anyway while our own currencies also depreciate.

By the way, I decided to elaborate a little more on this point in order to show that my approach to forecasting is deductive, that one idea builds on another.

5. *The inflation rate in the U.S. is around 8%.* What's the secondary effect?

Based on this fact, we know that investors who put their money in CDs (certificates of deposit) with a local bank earning a rate of 4% lose 4% per year.

People think savings accounts, CDs or long term U.S. treasuries or bonds are safe ways to preserve money. It isn't true! They are in fact some of the riskiest investments we can make. People lose anywhere from 2 to 6% every year depending on which of these "safe" options they go with and how much interest each pays.

There's another interesting fact we need to be aware of about government sponsored inflation. This fact explains why inflation is always at least double the official government figures. *Even if the inflation rate was 0%, Americans would still be paying an inflation tax.*

Here's my reasoning: In free markets, most prices fall year over year (I'm assuming about 1 to 4% per year). Prices are kept from falling because our government finances its debt by printing money, which in turn, increases costs.

The government isn't just taxing us on the *upside* (the inflation we do see) but also on the *downside* (on the deflation/savings we miss out on). Unless we know the natural rate of deflation, we can't really calculate the real rate of theft (inflation).

Inflation is the reason dual income American families today don't enjoy the same quality of life single earner families did in prior generations.

6. *More cars are being sold in China than in the United States.* What's the effect?

China is currently the largest car market in the world and growing. What does that mean? It means that China's industrialization in general will continue to grow at a rapid pace. As hundreds of millions of Chinese peasants join the middle class, China's energy needs will skyrocket. As this economic behemoth wakes up and starts to eat, oil prices will continue to climb. I predict that within a year or two, oil prices will go above $100/barrel.

China is the largest importer of Saudi Arabian oil, that trend will grow. China is expecting prices to rise—they must know something since they recently purchased a Canadian oil company this year at a price that required $90/barrel for them to be profitable. These are just the beginning signs of a surge in oil prices.

7. *The value of the dollar will depreciate against other currencies.* What's the effect?

This is also a fact of life. As developing economies continue to outpace the growth of the U.S. market, the price of their currencies will rise much faster than ours. As we experience low growth, other nations will grow faster. Some of the secondary effects of this fact are:

(a) The price of *all* imports will go up in cost because each dollar will be worth less.

(b) Foreigners (and Americans who invested in foreign equities) will be able to buy U.S. assets much cheaper than before.

(c) More foreigners will be able to vacation in the U.S.

(d) Less Americans will be able to vacation abroad.

8. *The worldwide debt crisis will continue and intensify.* What's the secondary effect?

This is also a fact. Recently, the Greek debt crisis caused a massive selloff of Europe's currency—the Euro. Ironically, Greece is a very small economy—too small for investors to get worked up about. What they're really concerned with is that the debt virus will spread to other countries that use the Euro.

However, investors are ignoring the U.S. debt situation which is far worse than what's happening in Europe. California, for example, is much bigger than Greece—it's the 8th or 9th largest economy in the world and it's on the brink of defaulting on its debts. California's not alone.

Just today I read that the city of Harrisburg (the capital of the state of Pennsylvania) might declare bankruptcy. The city missed its May interest payment of about $450,000. There are many cities, counties and states in worse shape than Harrisburg.

What does this fact indicate? A first thing this fact suggests is that investors will demand higher interest payments to invest in city, state or county bonds. During the Greek debt crisis, the interest investors demanded to lend Greece money skyrocketed to as much as 20%.

In the same way, interest charges will rise for states and cities all across the country, thereby increasing taxes and reducing benefits. Investing in state and municipal bonds was once considered a safe bet.

A second thing we can expect is a dramatic rise in gold prices. When people go for safety, they go for gold. Gold was naturally selected by free people and free markets as the currency of choice because it retained its value. If people had a choice, they'd always opt for gold—natural money.

Now as the debt crisis grows in the U.S., more people will seek safety in gold and gold prices will rise to about 1600 an ounce within 12-18 months.

9. *The Federal Government is offering an $8,000 tax credit for new homeowners and $6,500 for existing homeowners. What's the secondary effect?*

The unseen effect is a major tax on non-homeowners and homeowners that have purchased their homes before the credit was available. Renters all across the country should be very upset at this "bribe buyers out of the recession" scheme. Once again, as is the norm in the U.S., poor people are subsidizing wealthier folks (those who can afford a home).

A privilege for one group of people is always a liability for another because the government has no money. By its very nature, it can't give us anything we don't already have.

10. *China's savings rate is 45%. What's the secondary effect?*

Such a high savings rate affects different parts of the Chinese economy. Let's just look at how it affects their real estate market.

There has been speculation that a real estate bubble has formed in China. As I flip between three of my favorite financial networks CNBC, Bloomberg and CNBCW, I'll inevitably come across a fund manager who's worried about a possible real estate bubble in China.

I disagree that there's a bubble but even if there is, it won't be a problem for one reason: Their high savings rate creates a buffer against the consequences of bubbles. A bubble usually forms when everyone is buying on credit. Savings provide economic stability. With so much cash in the bank, Chinese homebuyers are not overleveraged. The Chinese authorities also require homebuyers to put up a cash down payment of between 20 and 50% in order to buy a home.

Property appreciation in China doesn't depend solely on the availability of debt (credit). It also depends on the availability of cash. So there's no bubble.

"I've found that when the market's going down and you buy funds wisely, at some point in the future you will be happy." ~Peter Lynch.

Can Anyone Be an Economist?

Kidus, I've been accused of having economic ideas that are "too neat and tidy" or "impossibly deductive." Some financial professionals think that telling people they can manage their own money is irresponsible because the financial markets are complex. But I'm a populist to the core, a supreme optimist in people's ability to achieve what they want if they have the time and energy to put in a little work.

Obviously, the more complicated the investment, the more facts we need to take into consideration; but if you've listened to anything I've said so far, we should run away from any investment a 12 year old can't understand.

For general investing purposes, and if people have the time, anyone can become a master money mechanic. It may take some time to learn all the parts of the investment vehicle we want to drive, but, it's worth the investment. Independent investors can learn how to do it themselves if they have time to do a little homework.

Even if we don't have enough time to actively manage our own money, we still need to know enough to decide whom to trust with our money. We squirrels have to do our best to protect our nuts. After all, brokers are not required by law to act in the best financial interests of their clients.

So let's assume we decide to manage our own money and choose to use the "neat and tidy" system of ideas presented here. In the long term, these ideas will benefit us.

However, short term market movements may seem to contradict our long term investment strategy. But just because something unexpected happens doesn't mean the world of economics isn't rational. Logic always retains its force and sooner or later people do come to their senses.

Warren Buffett's mentor, Benjamin Graham, once said that in the short term, the market is a voting machine, but in the long term, it's a weighing machine. Longer term predictions are always the safest, and, if they're based on sound ideas, eventually they'll come true.

Remember that thinking like a good economist is thinking about longer term effects. Another way to say it is that time is always on the side of a good bet if we can count the cards in the dealer's hand.

Buffett once said that time is always the enemy of a bad business but a friend of a good one. Time may not always feel like a friend. During his 2008 presidential campaign Ron Paul was laughed at. But all his predictions are coming true. Back in 2006, when Peter Schiff predicted almost every facet of the economic collapse (and even wrote a book about it) people thought he was crazy. They laughed at him; but he's got the last laugh.

Remember that unexpected or impossible things occur only in the short term; don't worry if you hit a rough patch. Keep studying the thoughts of Austrian economists, commentators and writers. Aristotle once said, "It's possible that the impossible happens". I'd add that "it's possible that the impossible happens but not for long"!

Markets do crazy things like buy up long term U.S. debt—but foolish acts will *eventually* produce disastrous consequences. Time always tells and its hand cannot be stopped. Either time is working for us or against us.

We know, for example, that time is working against U.S. fiscal solvency because, even by the government's projections (which are always understated), the federal budget deficit will reach $23 trillion dollars by 2019. Some economists have said that the debt can't be paid back. That $23 trillion doesn't take into account about $70 trillion of unfunded liabilities for Social Security, Medicare and other government programs.

America's growing debt resulted in a steady decline in the value of the dollar; investors made a rational decision to invest somewhere where they could better preserve their wealth. As the dollar is steadily declining to levels our "neat and tidy" philosophy is predicting, an unexpected occurs—a Euro selloff is sparked by Greek debt problems. Money that was in the Euro starts to flow back to the U.S. and thereby *temporarily* increases the price of the dollar beyond its real worth.

Does this Euro debt crisis or any other crisis change the fact the U.S. is broke? Of course not! In fact we even have short term reasons to believe that holding U.S. treasuries is a bad idea: Credit agencies have been threatening to downgrade the government's AAA rating. In short, think about the long term and the short term will make sense. There are no surprises.

Conclusion

These examples show us how to think about economic activity. The financial result of being able to *interpret* market activity is that when something (anything) happens in the marketplace, that activity becomes an opportunity.

91

Of course, we can't predict everything with certainty but we can become one of the best predictors in the market by simply using these ideas: (a) What I've called, "Newtonian method" or economic literacy; (b) by sticking with what we know; (c) by experimenting; (d) by following the leaders and, of course, (e) learning from history and mastering luck. Embrace your inner Newton!

Your Loving Uncle,
    Akinaw.

The One Thing You Must Understand

Dear Kidus,

For the last 12 years, something strange has been happening in Orange County, CA. For an unknown reason, residents have witnessed an epidemic of ugly babies being born to the most beautiful women in the world. Doctors were surprised at the frequency of these births. No one knew what was going on. Scientists feared pregnant women were being infected by Asiatic bacteria carried to the O.C. coast in ocean currents.

Then a researcher at U.C. Irvine found a gas emitting mineral deposit found only in Orange County. Was this the culprit? After further studies, they found that the gas was harmless. So what happened?

Researchers found that the only other O.C. epidemic on record was a sharp rise in the number of women getting plastic surgery. That craze had begun a little over 12 years ago. It turns out that the ugly baby epidemic was just the result of the false advertising plastic surgery had made available.

Okay, so the story isn't true. I'm simply advising you it's possible to mistakenly marry a bad investment without knowing it. The ugly baby that marriage produces tells you something is wrong.

Great Expectations

The U.S. economy has gone through lots of cosmetic surgeries, allowing it to distort what it really looks like. Understanding what things are really worth takes a little study but it will be worth it. It will save us a lot of heartache in the years to come.

Most financial mistakes occur because we don't know what things are really worth when we're at the altar saying our wedding vows. About 90% of investors falsely believe they know how to value assets. The reason some prices stay irrationally high or low for long periods of time is because enough buyers are acting on false premises.

Knowing how to value an asset is something every investor must understand extremely well. Real estate investors generally use comparable sales to determine the price of a property but that has obvious limits—there's a boom and bust every five years in real estate. That means that comparable sales in up markets will tell us values are higher but those same comparables will tell us prices are lower in down markets. Appraisers just state the obvious, there's no real rationale behind their valuations.

We need a better method of understanding what things are really worth. Comparable sales or our expectations of future value can disappoint us.

During the run up of real estate prices, I remember how everyone just expected prices to keep going up without ever giving a rational reason for that belief. Real estate was bought and sold on the dogmatic idea that prices just keep going up.

A lot of people bought into that idea and as a result, have lost their homes, their jobs and their trophy O.C. wives. A great deal of hurt, pain, confusion and anxiety can be avoided by doing some homework (this year alone, there will be 3 million foreclosure filings). If ever there was a time to understand how to value an asset, it is now! Both the banker and homebuyers need to understand this most important skill.

An investor's job is one thing and one thing only: To accurately judge the true value of an asset or an investment. In other words, "value investing" is the *only* investment methodology that we can use. Warren Buffett has been called a value investor. But there's no other way to invest.

Judging the true value of an asset or investment is made difficult by our Plastic Surgeon in Chief—the Federal Reserve System.

"I conceive that the great part of the miseries of mankind are brought upon them by false estimates they have made of the value of things." ~Benjamin Franklin.

For What it's Worth

I took a break from work last night to surf the web for financial news and watched an interview about whether real estate prices were still overvalued[1].

The economist being interviewed made some interesting comments on things other than real estate. He said that if we had bought *anything* in 1982 (bonds, real estate, stocks, etc.), we would've done very well on those investments (we'll see why in a minute).

When the discussion shifted to the arena of politics, he said that "the Austrians" (people with common sense economic views) are gaining popularity even though they have a history of being wrong about economic matters.

---

[1] http://www.huffingtonpost.com/2010/06/30/barry-ritholtz-housing-pr_n_631190.html

Now, I don't know what he's been smoking to say Austrians have a history of being wrong. Marijuana's legal in some states now so maybe he's smoking some *really* good stuff. After all, it's easy enough to go on YouTube.com and watch some of the recent predictions from the very mouths of Austrian economists like Peter Schiff he disagrees with. They've been right on just about *everything.*

You don't need to take my word for it, of course, and you don't have to scour the web to try to find their predictions. Other people have edited and compiled them for you. To see these predictions yourself, search, "Ron Paul and Peter Schiff were right" or "Peter Schiff Was Right" on YouTube.

Secondly, the reason any investment in 1982 would have done well (as he pointed out) is best explained by the very Austrian economists he mentions have a history of being wrong.

The reason all asset prices have gone up since 1982 is because *credit has increasingly grown since that time.* The graph below shows that interest rates have trended lower and lower since about 1982.

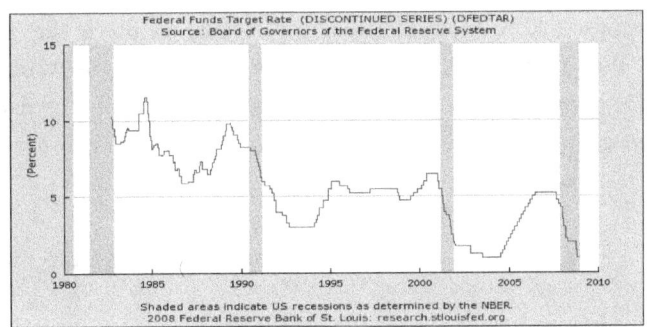

So how does this explain the huge rise of all investments since 1982?

Well, if interest rates are lowered, credit is made more available and people go shopping and everything *seems* to be worth more as a result. People use the available credit to buy up bonds, real estate, stocks, big cars, big homes, bigger lips, slimmer hips and of course, the bling bling. In other words, because more credit is available to more people, they all jointly bid up prices of all assets.

Everything seems to be more valuable but it's all a hoax. Just like the O.C. women I mentioned above, the American economy has been undergoing a great deal of plastic surgery since 1982. Instead of a scalpel, our economic surgeons use a printing press to create the *illusion* of prosperity.

This means that most assets in our economy are still overvalued and need to come down in price. I say this because all the liquidity that had been pumped into the system hasn't been taken back out. Assets are worth less than we may think because the market has been flooded with credit for a couple decades.

"You just have to be opportunistic, and try to figure out what creates value, where the bottom is, what creates incremental value, and in what combinations." ~John Malone.

Ugly Investments

Looking at past performance of stocks or real estate is a shoddy way to invest unless we understand the history behind the numbers. Otherwise, we might wake to find our investments are giving birth to ugly babies.

Lots of people are suckered into buying overvalued investments by looking at the past performance of markets without understanding *why* it's done so well.

Some think that if we're in the market long enough, any investment will appreciate. So the thinking is that if we held anything from 1982 until today, our investment would have appreciated, just because we put in the time.

Well that's not exactly true, we're not in a prison system—no one gets kudos for good behavior. If we look at the Dow Jones Industrial Average, there were *zero* gains from 1964 until 1981. In 1964 the average stood at 874, almost twenty years later, it was 875.

"Price is what you pay. Value is what you get." ~Warren Buffett.

What Every Investor Needs to Know

Unfortunately, most investors think that rising real estate or stock prices are either good *for* the economy or are rising *because* the economy is doing well.

But here's the thing everyone, and especially real estate investors, must understand: Rising prices of assets slowly destroy jobs. And if you know anything about real estate, jobs are the *most* important factor in creating the demand for real estate that's needed for sustainable appreciation.

To say that when asset prices go up, jobs are destroyed seems strange but it's a fact that's been acknowledged even by Federal Reserve economists. Here's how it works.

When asset prices (real estate, stocks) rise, so does our trade deficit. And huge trade deficits only mean one thing: Money and jobs are flowing *out* of our economy.

When a real estate investor sees prices go up as a result of the Fed's below market interest rates, she should slowly (1 to 3 years) get out of the market because as the rates go down, jobs and money will flow out of our economy. As wealth flows out, there will be fewer buyers available who can afford our properties in the long term. Of course, she may miss out on some appreciation at the top but she'll be in position to buy back in after the crash.

The huge trade deficit and the loss of jobs is why the real estate industry is having difficulty selling its excess inventory even though mortgage rates are at 50 year lows. Without jobs, buyers can't afford mortgage payments?

When prices are inflated, the equity in our homes and stock portfolios goes way up. But that growth is really a myth. Just like a rubber band, an economy returns to its original structure once we stop pulling one of its ends. Interest rates affect the value of assets in the same way. Low interest rates stretch the boundaries of our wealth beyond its true borders, making it look like we've got more than we do.

People then spend their savings, cash out some of their stocks or use the equity in their homes like a personal ATM. Saving and investment then goes down because people may feel they're closer to their financial goals as the equity in their homes or stock portfolios grow.

As a result of all this credit induced fake wealth (equity growth), our priorities shift from saving and production to borrowing and spending. The logic is this: "If I've got all this equity—all this wealth—I can take it easy for awhile. I don't have to save or be productive." Our industries begin to be dismantled and imports go up. The numbers show this scenario. *Since the early 1980s, the U.S. has run an ever increasing yearly trade deficit.*

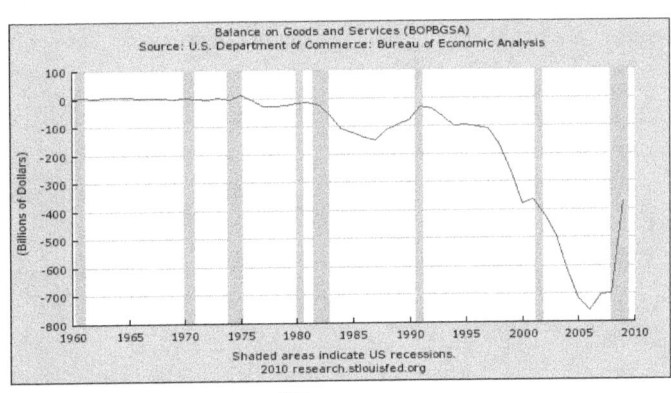

Look at the similarity between the artificially low interest rates (above) and increasing trade deficits.

If we put the two graphs side by side, they tell the same story. As the interest rates are *lowered*, the trade deficit *grows*. There's an inverse relationship between the two. That means our economy has been slowly drifting towards a day of reckoning as the *effects* of our loss of wealth and jobs catch up with us. We've been stretching the rubber band for decades and it's trying to snap back to its true dimensions.

Another interesting fact that we've pointed out in an earlier letter is that our economy only improves during recessions.

The graph above shows our trade deficit shrinks during recessions when credit contracts (shaded areas). We can also see that *sharp* recessions are better for our economy because the sharper the recession, the faster our trade deficit shrinks. The chart above shows that during our rather severe, current Squirrelspan recession, the deficit was cut in half from almost $800 billion per year to less than $400 billion.

So far so good right? But we seem to have a point that argues against the one I'm making.

"We are still masters of our fate. We are still captains of our souls." ~Winston Churchill.

The Bubble Economies

How come the value of all assets have gone up since 1982 if our trade deficit has been increasing (money has been flowing out) since that time? Surely, we should've seen the widening trade gap, become more sober minded as investors, pulled back a bit and calmed the upswing in prices. How come the unemployment rate was so low for so long if money was flowing out of our economy? We should expect asset prices to decrease if the economy has been losing jobs.

First, I should remind you that investors are hardly ever sober. In college, my classmates swore by a cure for a hangover: Drink more alcohol. I kid you not—people really believe that. I'm of the opinion that Wall Street believes the same thing.

Secondly, Americans have been spending their savings (real wealth) without knowing it. It's taken Alan Squirrelspan that long to get us to waste our store of nuts. We didn't recognize we were losing money and jobs because we started with a large amount of savings.

Thirdly, economies can go a long way by continually expanding credit. We don't always see the effects right away. We can go for years before an eventual bust.

Fourthly, even if one bubble bursts, we've learned to roll it over into new ones in other areas of the economy. After the dot com bust, for example, the money that flowed out of technology flowed into the real estate market (and other sectors).Wherever the ghost of bubbles past goes, it creates a new, false sense of economic growth. That false optimism creates jobs in that sector. Lots of jobs were created during the dot com bubble and millions more were created in the real estate industry before the eventual bust.

So even though we were, in reality, losing jobs for a long time, the credit bubbles have concealed that fact. Our economic bubbles created fake jobs on credit to compensate for the real ones we were losing. The longer we go without creating real jobs, the bigger the bubble gets. It all has to come back down to earth at some point. The excess credit can't shift from one bubble to another, building mass forever without popping. The longer the credit inflation continues, the bigger the eventual bust.

"I do not think it is an exaggeration to say history is largely a history of inflation, usually inflations engineered by governments for the gain of governments." ~Friedrich Von Hayek.

The Last Bubble

Government spending is another bubble that's been created to prop up our credit addicted economy. All the excess liquidity that's been building up since 1982 has now been transferred to the government's books. It has nowhere else to go. This is the biggest bubble of them all but it's a bit different than other bubbles. It can actually go for decades without bursting.

The government can go on spending beyond its means much longer than a homeowner is able to. The government is different because *we* are its equity. We are the State's *collateral*. All our work, joy, pain, hope, laughter and love can be crumbled up like wads of paper and thrown away because the reality of the matter is as long as our future can be borrowed against, we're all slaves.

If our lives, our future earnings and future standards of living can be *collateralized* like a home equity line of credit by the State, what else are we but slaves?

99

Sooner or later though, even the government must have ugly babies. We're at that point in Squirrelmerica. Social unrest is increasing and the government doesn't know what to do. They can kick the can down the road but not forever. The longer they postpone the inevitable, the worse our problems will become.

"Emancipate yourself from mental slavery, none but ourselves can free our mind."
~Bob Marley.

Uncle Sam's Schizophrenia

Now let me show how completely contradictory the government's actions are. You'll clearly see what can happen if you start a train of economic reasoning on false assumptions. In order to reduce the $13 trillion federal budget deficit, the government needs to collect more taxes; but it can only do so if jobs are being created. So, we can assume they want to create jobs. But they've got a problem. Real jobs can't be created if we've got annual trade deficits of $700 billion.

The problem is that the Fed, as Plastic Surgeon In-Chief (and silent partner with the Federal Government), keeps lowering interest rates to make the price of assets look higher, which then causes consumers to spend trillions on imported goods. *In this way, the government is fighting against its own goal of creating jobs!* The Fed should in fact be increasing interest rates to stop the outflow of jobs and money.

Look at the first graph above again. You can see that our economy is caught in something called "a debt trap". The interest rate graph looks like stair steps going down, always finding a new low. When the Fed tries to take the credit out of the system to avoid inflation, there's a recession and the central bank is again forced to pump in more money and the cycle is repeated. Remember that the Fed has created addicts (refer back to the "Central Dealer part in the letter on entrepreneurship) but now wants to outlaw drugs.

"Losing an illusion makes you wiser than finding a truth." ~Ludwig Borne.

Why the Fed Wants Higher Asset Prices

Our Fed Chairman, Ben Squirrelnanke, knows that allowing the economy to go into a deep depression will *quickly* cure all our economic problems but he'd be out of a job. All the debt we've accumulated can be liquidated. He doesn't want that to happen. Why? Well, because the Fed seems to only have one goal: *Making asset prices appreciate (as if that meant there's more wealth in the system) even if that contributes to an eventual loss of jobs, inflation and the destruction of our economy.*

I know this sounds strange but these are the facts. It doesn't sound so crazy when you remember that the Fed is a private organization created to serve big bank interests. The interest of banks since the beginning of time has always been to increase the amount of debt in circulation because the more that's lent, the more interest they can collect.

They must have such an ulterior motive because anyone can see how crazy it is to think an increase in the paper value of our assets means we're wealthier. From 1994 to 2004, the total net worth of American households doubled from about $23 trillion to $46 trillion. Was that real wealth creation or was it a result of ultra low interest rates that inflated prices beyond their real levels? That *huge jump in the value of household wealth coincides with historically low interest rates* (look at the graph again). It wasn't real. What *were* real were the bank profits all that fake wealth produced.

When you really think about what the Fed is really doing by basically shipping trillions of dollars to China and other Asian economies, you get the nagging suspicion Easy Al Squirrelspan and Ben Squirrelnanke are Chinese spies. After all, the correlation between money outflow and low interest rates is very obvious.

I recently read an article by an economist who was surprised to find out that a possible way to reduce our trade deficit and strengthen our economy was to lower the value of the equity in our homes. He shouldn't have been surprised.

"A great deal of intelligence can be invested in ignorance when the need for illusion is deep."
~Samuel Bellow.

The Credit Addiction Will End

As long as our economy is awash with credit, investors who don't understand how that affects the value of their long term investments will wake up one day with lots of ugly babies.

And when that happens, the plastic surgeon's response will be to perform even more surgeries to fool more investors. The only way to stop the ugly baby epidemic is to put down the scalpel—stop the money printing press. At least then, we can better predict what kinds of babies we'll have.

When I think about what's going on behind the scenes of our economy, I'm reminded of the story of Howard Hughes. When he was young, he was well kempt, dashing and dated the most beautiful movie stars of his day. But after suffering massive injuries in a nearly fatal plane crash, his life changed.

He slowly became addicted to pain relieving drugs. As the addiction grew, it also worsened the obsessive compulsive disorder he'd partially kept under control until that time. For years, he locked himself away in dark hotel rooms, at times sitting naked in one spot for months. His hair, nails, beard all grew long and mangled.

When he died, the autopsy revealed a bony, scraggly, disheveled old man whose body was full of dope and whose arms had multiple needles broken off in his veins.

That's a picture of what's happening to the American economy. Our drug of choice is credit and that drug triggers *our* compulsive disorder—spending. The spending in turn makes us even more dependent on more credit. And that transfers even more wealth to foreign economies as our trade deficits continue to grow.

For years, it was thought cheap, overseas labor was the reason our trade deficits kept increasing. Those two graphs above prove that the problem is our own. We're one of few nations running a trade deficit with China, they're not to blame.

"Paper is poverty….it is not money, but the ghost of money." ~Thomas Jefferson.

What Can a Brotha Do?

Kidus, here are a few ways to use this information for investing purposes if you get to the States:

- Understand that real estate appreciation depends on job growth and that huge trade deficits slowly ship money and high paying manufacturing jobs overseas. For this reason, the real estate problem will continue for years. So it doesn't matter if rates on mortgages stay below 5%; if jobs aren't being created, you can't expect real property appreciation. Think about investing in real estate overseas. Find partners, investment vehicles (such as REITS) and deals in China, Mexico, India, etc.

- Stay out of the real estate market until Uncle Sam leaves it alone. Recently, there was a huge drop in real estate sales as the "Bribe Buyers at the Expense of Renters" tax credit program ended. We shouldn't be surprised of course because when you give buyers an incentive to buy now rather than later, you're simply carrying demand forward. There's always a limited amount of buyers in the marketplace at any given time, when you upset that ratio through tax credit schemes (easy credit does this as well), quick up and down price swings is the result. Who knows what the government will come up with next? Like most real estate investors, I want to flip properties but it's too risky, so I'm doing something else.

- Don't buy domestic stocks. Stocks of U.S. based companies are overvalued and will be so as long as the trade deficit continues to grow and interest rates continue downward. Trade deficits are a better indicator of our economy's health than the price of assets. As long as the government pushes people to spend instead of save and invest, our economy will slowly sink into a pit. If I could ask you to remember one thing from this letter, it's that spending is at the root of our problems because most of what we buy comes from overseas.

- Invest your money overseas or in commodities. Massive amounts of money will be printed to sustain artificially high prices of assets in the U.S. as Ben Bernanke will do his best to ruin our economy.

- Don't invest in U.S. Treasuries or government bonds. If rates stay down for a long time, remember that inflation and the collapse of the value of the dollar will be the inevitable result. If the Fed acts responsibly and rates go way up to calm inflation, the price of bonds will collapse.

- Stay away from investing in most industrialized nations as they'll experience much less growth than their Asian and Latin American counterparts. Comparing the two is like placing the young, dashing Howard Hughes alongside the long bearded, mangy, drug addicted one. Debt has a way of destroying wealth. Europe, Britain and the United States are in the middle of a debt crisis because they've slowly become credit addicted welfare states.

- Make sure that your investment perspective is at least 10-20 years out. It can take a long time for us to see the consequences of government action. It took us 25 years to feel the consequences of credit growth. Knowing what things are worth takes a little bit of detective work and

103

it's easy to fall in love with that beautiful investment. Therefore, understand that it's possible that our economy can go through another "decade of zero growth". Fed chairman Ben Squirrelnanke is doing his best to stop our economy's recovery by injecting more drugs (credit) into our economy's veins.

- Be skeptical but optimistic. Nietzsche once said that if you stare into an abyss long enough, it will stare back at you. In a similar way, I've found that if I focus on what the government and its central planners are doing to our economy, I'll find the truth about what things are really worth. That makes me a better investor. We can't be great investors without understanding how the economic policies at the top affect our livelihoods.

- You can still make money by quickly getting in and out of the market. If you've got the cash, you can still buy and sell real estate to make some money. You can't get greedy and you've got to be quick.

Kidus, I know it seems like the government creates a horrendous environment in which to create wealth but that doesn't mean it makes it impossible. The information you've received isn't meant to discourage ambition but to give it a ground on which to stand. It will save you a great deal of disappointment and disillusionment later on if you don't look at these things now. Reality is just reality—the sooner we can understand it, the sooner our financial lives will improve.

Being realistic doesn't mean you can't be optimistic—it just means you have to have good reasons for it.

Your Loving Uncle,
    Akinaw.

Part Three

The Secrets of

Capital Management

Riches to Rags

Dear Kidus,

Wealthy people are not just born, they're made. Even if some of them inherit their wealth, preserving it takes some skill. To get the most from the following letters, you must realize that 90% of capital management is the preservation of capital; the other 10% is growing it.

The rich create their riches through wealth consciousness—by learning the art of building and preserving wealth. Building wealth is an art that must be learned through experience and education. It rarely, if ever, just comes naturally. One of the most fascinating things about self-made wealthy people is how important a role an entrepreneurial parent played in their success.

If you were to pick up a copy of Forbes magazine's richest people list, you'll notice 9 out of 10 had entrepreneurial parents. This shows that wealthy people pass on more than just money—they pass on the *knowledge* of how to make it and keep it.

Of course, every other social class passes intellectual capital from one generation to another. The talk around the dinner table of a welfare family is how to get more welfare checks. Middle class families tend to talk about getting jobs or job security. The wealthy, on the other hand, talk about business, investing or politics.

Just like animals, human parents teach their kids how to hunt different types of prey. Whether a child learns how to apply for welfare or how to start a profitable business, they're getting an education—they're receiving *capital*. They earn *an amount of interest that corresponds to the skill or know-how they've learned from their parents* or their environment.

Wealthy people, for example, don't outsource investing knowledge to so called 'experts'. Instead, they learn what to do with their money as they grow up. Kids of poor parents, on the other hand, don't learn how to handle money or understand how to value assets.

If you were to give a million dollars to someone who's never had money training, you can be sure it'll be blown away in a heartbeat. Lottery winners, for example, usually find themselves back where they were within a few years. Or better yet, think about former boxing champ and ex-multimillionaire Leon Spinks.

Below is a Boston Globe story about him titled, *"Riches to Rags."* As you read this short story, see if you can recognize a trend:

"The years have been tough. Spinks got divorced and lived briefly in an East St. Louis shelter. He was a greeter at Mike Ditka's restaurant in Chicago. He says he helped start a gym in Detroit and did odd jobs in California. Now he cleans the local YMCA for $5.15 an hour on weekends, sometimes unloads trucks at McDonald's, and volunteers to help the homeless. The Champ also likes his second job at the local McDonald's. "I get 50 percent off on Big Macs and everything," he said. Spinks also goes to several autograph shows each year. Three of Spinks' sons followed in their father's footsteps and became professional fighters. Leon, the eldest, was murdered in St. Louis in 1993. Darryl had 20 professional fights, and their younger brother, Cory, born just five days after his father beat Ali, is a former welterweight champion. Spinks, who was arrested in April 1978 for cocaine possession, is told that the public perception of him is that he partied away the nearly $5 million he made from fighting. "That's [expletive]," he said. "That's what people think. I was stupid and I gave [the lawyers] power of attorney." He says he never saw a penny of the $3.75 million he made for the Ali-Spinks 2."[2]

Sad right? Despite the title of the article being "Riches to Rags", Spinks was never really rich to begin with because riches are always a product of a state of mind. He never had a millionaire mind—he had the mind of a minimum wage worker who could throw a good punch.

Did you notice the career paths all three of his sons chose? Spinks didn't push them into what naturally turned into the family biz.

The truth is, in a lot of cases, kids follow in the footsteps of their parents because it's the easiest way to acquire intellectual capital—the know-how to produce a product or service to meet their needs.

But unfortunately, as cynical as it may sound, the following generations (even if they learn how to make millions from boxing) still may not know-how to save money, invest wisely, or as may have been the case for Spinks, know how to deal with legal contracts and lawyers.

Why I want to teach capital management is because it's easy to allow the misconceptions of the crowd and the economically illiterate to affect our

---

[2] http://www.boston.com/sports/other_sports/boxing/articles/2005/12/21/riches_to_rags

financial future. Our society has spiritual sons in the same way that Spinks had sons. Society procreates thought forms—people. The beauty of knowledge is that you can give birth to yourself. "As a man thinketh", said Solomon, "so is he." The promise of that proverb is that you can be what you think. Thinking correctly about capital is foundational to creating the financial life you desire.

"Education is the transmission of civilization." ~Will Durant.

Your Loving Uncle,
    Akinaw.

Be Like Grace

Dear Kidus,

Entrepreneurship has always been in my blood. Before coming to the U.S. at the age of 8, I watched my mother run a home based business. She didn't answer phones or knit sweaters, instead she served homemade alcohol in a make shift bar carved out of our living room.

As a single mother, she did the best she could but selling alcohol came with its obvious dangers. Unsavory men were coming in and out of the house at late hours of the night. Imagine the kind of nerve and toughness it took to run such a business with a young child in the house.

Because there were no male relatives in the house at times, some of those nights were a bit scary. I remember one experience very vividly. A man was sitting at the bar table drinking one shot after another by candlelight (we had no electricity). He slowly became very intoxicated. He began to run his fingers through a candle flame.

The bearded drunk kept running his fingers through the flame, mumbling incoherent jargon until he knocked a candle over. He began to curse and yell at the candle. He seemed to be getting increasingly violent. He was losing control of his movements. At that point, my mother encouraged him to leave—but only after payment for his last few drinks.

He grumbled, staggered to the door, stepped outside and, for some reason, just stopped. He turned around and wouldn't let my mother close the door. I was terrified because I intuitively knew he didn't want to come back in just to have another drink.

All of a sudden, my mother took an empty alcohol bottle she had in her right hand and smashed it down on his head. The bearded menace fell backwards like a tree, flat on his back. He was knocked out cold. My mother calmly closed the door and to this day, I don't know how long he remained unconscious at our doorstep before staggering home. What I do know is that my mother and I slept with three eyes open—her two and my one.

"Through the humbling dispensations of Divine Providence, men are sometimes fitted for his service." ~John Woolman.

Lessons Learned

That experience taught me some very valuable lessons about money.

First, money isn't always easy to make. Sometimes you risk everything to get so very little, just as my mother had done to provide me with food and shelter. Accumulating capital can be a rough, gritty, experience if you're doing it in the wrong environment.

Second, making just enough money to live another day is a cyclical, hand to mouth existence. My mother had to sell more liquor to more strangers night after night in order to keep bread on the table.

But the most important lesson came after I'd been in the U.S. for twenty years—the purpose of making money is to buy time and freedom. Every dollar you earn must be strategically saved and invested so that it earns enough dividends/interest to pay for your living expenses. *Passive income should be the first and most important goal of any financial plan.*

My mother didn't have a business plan; she never received a business education but she understood this principle intuitively. When I was six years old, my job was shepherding the one family cow we owned. Years later, when I returned to Ethiopia for a visit, my mother had about a dozen cows she was renting to other farmers. She was also renting our first home, she was receiving passive income.

Billions of people around the world must work so very hard to get so little. But because a great amount of wealth has been accumulated in the Western world, making a great living is much easier. *Squirrelmerica's nut forests have more trees in them because previous generations of squirrels have planted them.*

Lastly, I've learned we should save much more when times are good. Money can flow out of an economy just as easily as it can flow in. Wherever it goes, it produces jobs and income. Capital is fluid. It's not stagnant. It moves, it's borderless.

The total net worth of an economy changes depending on the collective action of its inhabitants. If previous generations of Squirrelmericans had not been savers and producers, their children would not have the bountiful prosperity they now see. A lot of people think our wealth in the Western world will endure. But that's not necessarily true. There have been over 4,000 civilizations on record but each one has collapsed.

Central management of Squirrelmerica's economy can only succeed in destroying the available store of nuts in its economy. I've already shown how government and the Fed only contribute to the deforestation of nut trees in the

Squirrelmerica story. We know that a foolish squirrel can squander its own inheritance but government is the only thing that can make foolish squirrels of us all. Remember that the squirrels ate a lot of their nut inheritance because they were misled into thinking the forest trees were producing an abundant harvest.

"If you would be wealthy, think of saving as well as getting." ~Ben Franklin

Saving and Success

Saving does more than just give us the seed money to compound our returns. We can also duplicate ourselves.

One benefit of passive income is freedom from all sorts of anxiety. When you relieve yourself of anxiety, you're more productive because you can stop and think about opportunities. Not having to worry about where your next meal will come from buys you the time to come up with creative ways of making greater amounts of money.

Psychologist Mihaly Csikszentmihalyi (I thought *my* name was difficult) has shown in his book, *Creativity*, that creativity comes from a *surplus of attention*. Poor people don't have a surplus of attention because with every passing hour they're on the edge of economic ruin. They have no time to invest in themselves. People in the middle and lower classes have a huge disadvantage because large sums of money are only paid to people who create ideas. Without breathing space, you can't come up with good money making ideas.

I've heard that Apple CEO Steve Jobs came up with the idea of the Ipod at a meditative retreat. That doesn't surprise me. If Jobs was broke, running from one job to another to make ends meet, he wouldn't have come up with the perfect idea. The habit of saving does more than just compound interest; it also unleashes our creative imagination to create wealth out of thin air. It allows us to compound our brain.

Unfortunately, many people go to bed every night not knowing how they'll be able to provide food and shelter for their children. Every day thousands of people go to work injured because they have no other way of paying for food and rent. Most of these people will never have five minutes to devote to creating a way out of the cycle (it's up to their friends and family to interrupt them).

There are only two ways to get out of the trap: 1) Save and 2) Make money. The art of capital management starts with saving your nuts and compounding returns (planting nut trees). All the other concepts we'll learn (such as inflation, Social Security, gold, stock markets, currencies, taxes, etc.) are all designed to help you do just two things with your money: save it and grow it.

"The wise man saves for the future but the foolish man spends whatever he gets."
~Proverbs 21:20.

Simple and Time Tested

The art of saving is the starting point of financial success. We can't become independently wealthy without making a commitment to save. In the history of mankind, no one has ever achieved lasting prosperity without saving.

Getting to the pinnacle of financial success is accomplished only through a spirit of frugality. Consider the famous Warren Buffett. His first rule of business is "Don't lose money", his second rule is "Don't forget rule number one." His car license plate even reads "Mr. Thrifty". What more evidence do we need that prosperity is a result of under consumption (savings) and wise money management?

But you may think Mr. Buffett created his billions because he's a trained investor who understands the world of high finance. Can the art of saving produce any real results for the average person?

First of all, Buffett is a brilliant investor but his success is more a result of character and temperament than just intelligence. His mentor, Benjamin Graham, once said that anyone with the right character can earn high returns because intelligent investing isn't just about brains. As long as you can develop the right character within yourself, you too can accomplish the same things others have.

"Empty pockets never held anyone back. Only empty heads and empty hearts can do that."
~Norman Vincent Peale

Be Like Grace

To prove to you that saving is a golden path to prosperity for just about anyone, I'd like to introduce you to a secretary who turned $180 into $7 million. Her name was Grace Groner.

In 1935, she purchased stock in a company (Abbott Laboratories) worth $180. Having lived through the Great Depression, Grace learned the value of saving, whenever her stock paid dividends, she reinvested the money by buying more shares of stock. Year after year, she continued with the habit of re-investing her profits as she continued working as a secretary.

Her initial $180 soon turned into a million, then two million and finally ballooned to over $7 million. Grace didn't abruptly quit her job as a secretary when she became a millionaire. She stayed at her job for 43 years.

She didn't live a lavish life. Instead, she shopped for clothes at second hand stores, walked to work instead of buying a car, and although she could've owned any property in the city of Lake Forest, she lived in a one-bedroom house. Grace received more joy from giving than from spending. Throughout the years, her giving enabled numerous students to study abroad even as she continued to save.

Her friends said that she just had a knack for saving money and finding deals. So her money grew until it snowballed into a fortune.

When she donated $7 million to a local college, the size of her fortune surprised everyone—including her closest friends and relatives. No one expected a secretary to become a multi-millionaire—it defied conventional thought. But it defied the conventional thinking of people who are in the habit of spending all they earn.

Savers like Warren Buffett, I'm sure, are not surprised that saving leads to automatic wealth creation. There's no other way to build and maintain wealth. *Once we begin to save, invest and reinvest dividends, we realize the powerful effect of compounding interest.* We see our wealth grow without having to work to make it happen.

"The waste of money cures itself, for soon there is no more to waste." ~M.W. Harrison

Why People Don't Save

In order for us to build this all-important habit, we must decide what's important to us—we must understand how we relate to money.

The inability to save for most people results from a limiting belief of some kind. Some people with self-worth issues, for example, give the money away because they don't feel they deserve it. We can never have something we don't feel we deserve.

When I was training salespeople, I remember that one of my trainees would successfully convince a prospect to buy a product but then hang up before asking for payment.

Others use money to alleviate whatever anxiety is in their hearts. But I've come to learn that whatever we use to alleviate our anxiety eventually turns on us and becomes another source of anxiety for which a new drug must be found.

Know thyself and be at peace. Grace Groner was fulfilled in her relationships with her family and friends. It was that fulfillment that allowed her to save—a value she learned living through the Great Depression.

Both Grace and Buffett share the characteristic of contentment. When I was watching a documentary about Buffett, I remember hearing someone describing him as "content". He still lives in the same house he's been in for decades. He doesn't wear flashy clothes or drive a Rolls Royce.

Howard Hughes, America's first billionaire, drove a beat up car around the streets of LA. One day his publicist got in the beat up old car and asked him, "Howard, if you can afford any car you want, why do you drive this beat up old thing?" Hughes turned to him and said, "What do I have to prove?"

No wealth or security can be had if you don't save. Remember always Benjamin Franklin's words: "The way to wealth is industry and frugality."

"Contentment makes poor men rich; discontentment makes rich men poor."
~Benjamin Franklin

The Advantage of American Prosperity

Having experienced poverty for the first eight years of my life, I understand the real advantage of American prosperity. It's just one thing: *American citizens have the ability to save and invest enough money to buy their time and economic freedom within a relatively short amount of time compared to the rest of the world.*

For over thirty years, my mother struggled to sell enough liquor, to buy enough cows to rent to enough farmers to retire, to be able to live just outside the gates of poverty. Thirty years!

Americans need not struggle as long as she had to, in order to retire (and do so with much more dignity than is afforded her). However, the time Americans have to be able to save is slowly running out.

America is still one of the wealthiest countries in the world but that distinction may be coming to a close for reasons most people do not yet see. Any genuine economist who's not bought by a special interest will tell you that the economy won't be getting any better for awhile. The long term structural problems are much worse than the current recession.

There's no denying that the trees in Squirrelmerica's forests are not producing as many nuts as they used to. We must admit this reality in order to understand a crucial point: We must save all the nuts we can now and plant new trees so that we'll have an adequate supply in the future.

This means that two groups especially—the middle class and baby boomers—have a short window of opportunity (5 to 10 years) to save and invest their way to financial security. We must remember that our government's economic policies have been slowly shutting the doors to financial freedom for almost 100 years. It's all about to come to a horrible conclusion. The more they do, the harder it will become to preserve what wealth remains in the system.

Every government program that's been set up to guarantee our financial security has been used to enrich the few and impoverish the many. All of these programs from Social Security to Medicare are all bankrupt. There's less financial security in the United States as a result of these programs than ever before.

Our *total* unfunded debt is over $100 trillion. For the first time in our history, a child born in the U.S. must declare bankruptcy by their first birthday because they'll owe over $1 million dollars as soon as they're born. America's future generations will be born into economic slavery. There are 40 million people on food stamps, more than at any other time in Squirrelmerican history.

Our government promised Americans paradise if we gave it control over our lives. We took the bait and are now facing a harsh financial desert.

"I'm living so far beyond my income that we may almost be said to be living apart."
~E.E Cummings

Hidden Mines

But all of this is the bright side of our economic future. There are other reasons why saving will be more difficult in the years to come.

One hidden mine that's about to burst is the coming shortage of commodities (like energy and materials). As the economies of developing nations grow, the prices of all commodities from oil, gas, gold, copper and raw materials will rise dramatically.

China is already the largest importer of Saudi Arabian oil. And as I said before, Middle East nations would rather do business with China than with the U.S. because of what one Saudi prince referred to as "relational baggage" which he attributed to our intervention in the affairs of Arab states. In other words, we don't have "energy security" if the people we depend on for oil have both a grudge *and* another cash rich buyer.

As oil and other commodity prices rise, so will the costs of just about everything else. If wheat prices go up, so will cereal. If oil prices go up, gas prices do too. In fact, high oil prices increase the cost of every product in the global economy. As these prices increase, Americans will have less money to save.

Of course, we've been broke for over 25 years but no one has cared because our credit was still good. We charged everything onto our *credit* card by monetizing our debt (printing money). But the rest of the world is on to our scheme. The perception of American economic invincibility is being shattered.

The U.S. Treasury is having difficulty selling enough bonds to finance government expenses. I remember watching a show once and finding out that the Fed was buying billions of dollars of Treasury notes when there were no other buyers. One commentator then asked, "Isn't that a Ponzi scheme?"

That's exactly what it is. Our government is engaged in the biggest Ponzi scheme in history. How can the government sell Treasury notes to itself? What this tells us is that people don't want our debt as much as they did at one time. So buying increasingly expensive imports on credit will come to an end much sooner than we realize.

If more and more of our incomes become devoted to paying for food and energy, we'll have less capital to save and invest. And therefore, we'll be just another step closer to the constant dread of a hand to mouth existence that people in third world countries experience every day.

Secondly, there's a final problem we need to be aware of: How is the government going to pay for over $100 trillion of unfunded liabilities? Here are its options: (1) Reduce benefits (e.g., raise social security eligibility age 70 or even 75); (2) Raise taxes; (3) Print a huge amount of money.

Regardless of how the government pays for its debts, American standards of living will be reduced in the process. Our out of pocket costs will increase. Squirrelmericans will be living from nutcheck to nutcheck much longer than they'd have to were it not for Uncle Sam. This is an important reason to save *now*.

Third, as our government prints more dollars to cope with its debt, each dollar will be worth less. Costs for everything from gas, oil, iron, copper and food will increase. These increases will be far more costly as a percentage of income for the middle class and the poor than the rich.

Fourth, as the rest of the world develops, we won't have the advantage of cheap labor to subsidize our living standards. Chinese workers, who have subsidized our lifestyle by keeping inflation low, are going on strike for more pay. As their salaries increase, our imports will become more expensive. Once again, this will be a greater burden for the middle class who have less disposable income to afford the cost increases.

All these trends will basically create a caste system for those who do not *understand* the importance of saving. Never in Squirrelmerica's history has saving nuts for the winter been so important. Your job is to make as much money as you can now, save as much of it as possible and invest those savings wisely while the doors to financial freedom are still open.

However, the doors of prosperity always remain open to people who are economically literate. Nothing is too hard for us to overcome through education. The following story is a great example of this.

Although George Washington Carver was born a slave, he ended up working with the famous Henry Ford and became an agricultural advisor to three presidents: Calvin Coolidge, Theodore Roosevelt and Franklin Roosevelt. His research, patents and innovations led to hundreds of products that we enjoy today—dyes, axle grease, soy milk, peanut butter, cosmetics and hundreds of other uses for peanuts, soy and sweet potatoes. He also discovered that crop rotation would help the agricultural output of southern farmers. His story shows that it doesn't matter how bad things get in the economy, we'll never start out in the type of conditions Carver was born into.

His advice to us is this: "There is no short cut to achievement. Life requires through preparation—veneer isn't worth anything." Let's heed his words and remember that our economic conditions are as useless in keeping us from *our* dreams as slavery was from keeping Carver from his. Thorough preparation isn't easy but it pays the best dividends.

Your loving Uncle,
    Akinaw.

Golden Gloves and
Golden Records

Dear Kidus,

I hope you see why I said it's easier to become wealthy than it is to be rich. People who have invested the time to understand how the economy works and where it's headed are wealthy.

In my last letter, for example, I've shown that understanding the global context helps us see why we should save. Others like Grace Groner have learned, by living through the Great Depression, the importance of saving as well as finding contentment in people rather than possessions.

Being rich, on the other hand, does not depend on education or experience. It usually depends on unusual characteristics, natural talents, constant work or just pure luck. Lottery winners, movie stars, professional athletes and performers are rich. Sports team owners, record label owners, and movie producers are wealthy.

There are more rich people in the U.S. than anywhere else in the world. It's easier to get rich here than anywhere else in the world but I've noticed that rich people seem to end up broke. And to my surprise, it doesn't matter how much money rich people make, they'll find a way to blow it away.

Magic Castles

Actor Nicolas Cage, for example, has made almost $4 billion dollars throughout his career as an actor—an unimaginable amount of money for most people to even grasp. Think about the interest that amount of principal would generate.

When I was in college, I remember talking to my friends about how hard it would be to spend the interest on a billion dollars. We thought it would be impossible.

We used to talk about rich people and calculate the interest they'd make on their money. We would say things like, "Do you realize that if Bill Gates spent $50 million every month for the rest of his life, he'd never go broke?"

Well, I've learned that it doesn't matter how much money you have, it's possible to go broke.

Even though Nicolas Cage made such a staggering amount of money, he's blown a lot of it away. His mansions in California, Las Vegas and New Orleans are going into foreclosure and in order to pay his debts (including $20 million he owes the IRS), he's forced to sell his other assets in a recession—at enormous discounts. He unsuccessfully tried to sell his Bel Air mansion a year ago for $35 million. He put the same property back up on the market this year for $10.4 million but there were no bidders!

So where did all the money go? What's the cause of his financial woes? How can you possibly spend billions by the age of 45? Here's are some clues:

1. 18 motorcycles and 50 cars including Ferrari's, Lamborghinis, and nine Rolls Royces.
2. A Gulf Stream Jet.
3. Four yachts.
4. 15 enormous mansions in Bel Air, Las Vegas, Newport Beach, New Orleans and other places.
5. Two islands in the Bajamas!
6. A $1.6 million comic book collection.
7. And don't forget castles in Germany and England.

You may be tempted to think that Mr. Cage's financial problems resulted from his spending but it's not that simple. It wasn't his *spending* but *what* he was spending that dragged him to financial ruin.

There's one thing that wealthy people know *never* to spend: their principal! Spending your principal is giving up your freedom, something wealthy people see as the road to financial ruin.

"Too many people spend money they haven't earned, to buy things they don't want, to impress people they don't like." ~Will Smith

Golden Gloves and Golden Records

Despite making over $500 million throughout his career, famed boxer Mike Tyson is broke. Iron Mike didn't understand money, so he spent his principal.

Mike spent his principal on a $14 million mansion in Connecticut that he was eventually forced to sell. The man who now sleeps in that mansion is rap star 50 Cent.

The irony of this story is that both of these men are entertainers; but the one who's kickin' it in Mike's old crib isn't rich—he's wealthy. The only difference I could see between them was their perspective on money.

50 Cent recently appeared on TV to promote a book he'd co-written—the *50th Law*. During the interview, I was fascinated to learn that this guy is no ordinary, rich entertainer.

He said that living in a mansion that once belonged to someone who made over $500 million in his boxing career, is a daily reminder to always live below his means. What he's saying of course is that he doesn't spend his principal—*there's no other way to live below your means*. The true definition of saving is *under-consumption*, living below our means.

What makes *50 Cent* even more remarkable is his exceptional business sense. *He respects capital*. A few years back, he invested $10 million in Vitamin Water, used his celebrity status to promote it and earned an *after-tax* profit of $100 million when the company was sold to Coca-Cola.

When I saw him in the Vitamin Water commercials, I thought he was just another rich entertainer working for someone else—I had no idea he owned his own ideas, his own brands and wrote his own checks.

Now, I'm not surprised that someone who's good at capital management would also be a good entrepreneur. Good habits have a way of attracting other good habits. The great thing about building wealth is that we can start the process through any of the four principles I've identified as being the only paths to financial prosperity. Just start with your strength.

I said in one of my earliest letters that the four principles of wealth creation are interrelated. *50 Cent's* story is a clear example of it.

He used talent, drive and hard work to produce popular songs (productivity); then he saved his money by living below his means (capital management); and lastly, by investing his savings in Vitamin Water, he experimented his way to a $100 million after-tax profit (entrepreneurship).

Guess what he's up to now? Having mastered music, beverages and book publishing, he's now learning the movie production business. None of this would have been possible if he hadn't learned to save, without living below his means.

"A word to the wise ain't necessary—it's the stupid ones that need the advice." ~Bill Cosby.

No Need for Extremes

As I've grown older, I've lost control of my bowels. No, I'm kidding—just wanted to see if you're paying attention. But seriously, growing older has taught me some important things. I've become an extremist about saving money. I see ways to save money today that I'd never thought of when I was younger because I understand how savings fits into the structure of nutconomic activity.

A great way to save *a lot* of money is to *not* overpay for an asset (real estate, stocks, bonds, etc.). Buying in a bubble is always a danger. That's why I showed you how to value an asset through the letters on economic literacy. Then I showed you how to value an asset through the principle of economic literacy.

The real estate crash taught me a lot about asset valuation. I learned in the words of Milton the poet, how "few sometimes may know, when thousands err." I've taken the time to learn what it is that the few know.

I've slowly and painstakingly become a nutconomic expert because I *never* want to overpay for any asset or get stuck in a nutconomic recession.

In addition to reading voraciously, I also listen to countless audio files whenever I drive anywhere—the grocery store, to work, when I took a break, or went to sleep. I read until my eyes burned. And because I was thinking about economics every minute of the day, I even dreamt about it. One night, I had a dream that I was advising Obama on how he should responsibly spur growth based on the four principles of wealth creation.

Another night, I dreamt that four cobra snakes were dancing together in my living room. Each snake was a different color but they were all dancing in unison and headed in the same direction (four principles). Snakes are a symbol of healing. My subconscious was giving me positive feedback about *Wealthology*.

But you don't need to go to such lengths to learn every aspect of our nutconomy. I do all that work because it's what I love. In order to craft my skills in being a successful investor and lay a solid foundation as a fund manager, the *one* thing I must do better than 99% of people on earth is know how much assets are really worth at any given time.

Most people don't need to know as much to be prosperous (if what little they do know is learned accurately). Remember that Grace Groner was a lifelong secretary. Although she wasn't an expert economist, she had one thing most others didn't—commitment and discipline. That commitment produced a financial snowball.

Giving up momentary comforts is worth getting to a place where you can experience the magic of compounding interest. If we must resort to buying day old bread, used clothes, or moving into a cramped studio apartment in a "not-so-good part of town" to start the automatic capital accumulation process, we should do so. It's worth it. John D. Rockefeller was right to say, "Compounding interest is the 8th wonder of the world."

Most people need not go to extremes to get their passive, interest/dividend income to exceed their living expenses; all they must do is reduce their expenditures and invest the savings wisely.

When I was 19 I began working for Citigroup marketing financial products. As part of our sales pitch, we'd illustrate the magic of compounding interest by calculating the long term effect of cutting out their daily cup of coffee from their budget and instead investing that money at a 10% growth rate.

People are surprised at how much money that adds up to. Assume that someone buys a $4 cup of coffee every other day. That comes out to $728 spent on coffee every year. Here's how the math works:

1. $728/year for 20 years.
2. At 10% compounding rate.
3. Total in 20 years: $50,763.44!

"Beware of little expenses; a small leak will sink a great ship." ~Benjamin Franklin.

Anatomy of a Millionaire

In my twenties, one of the few members of my family who encouraged my entrepreneurial drive was my cousin Ken. Every Christmas or Thanksgiving, he'd either give me a financial book, let me borrow his or tell me to go pick up a copy myself if he thought I should read it.

One of these books was *The Millionaire Mind* by Thomas J. Stanley, Ph.D. It's based on a national survey of 733 millionaires (households that had *at least* a net worth of $1 million). The findings are interesting because the study sample was so large. So what did this exhaustive study find out about the average millionaire's perception of money?

Answer: They're extremely frugal.

Instead of buying new furniture, they get old ones reupholstered. Instead of buying new shoes, they get them resoled; instead of buying indiscriminately, they shop from lists, buy home supplies in bulk and even clip coupons. The frugality extends to recreation as it does to making buying decisions.

In their spare time, while the middle class is blowing their paycheck at a bar or at the mall, most millionaires don't spend a dime. In their spare time, 86% of the 733 millionaires said they planned their investments. Seventy eight per cent said they researched investment opportunities.

We don't have to deprive ourselves in order to become financially independent. If we use your mind, we can create a balanced approach that'll get us where we want much quicker than we thought possible. We can either be a Mike Tyson or 50 Cent—it's all a matter of perspective.

It's amazing how fast later comes when you buy now! ~Milton Berle

Your Loving Uncle,
Akinaw.

What's Your Store of Value?

Dear Kidus,

One of the risks of creating business ideas is being copied by imitators. If you were to visit downtown LA's Fashion District, you'd see a lot of imitators. But what I once discovered was that they're not even that good at imitating.

Years ago, I bought a copy of Michael Jackson's *Thriller* album from a street vendor in LA. I opened it, popped it in my car's CD player and couldn't believe what I heard. Michael Jackson was singing in a Puerto Rican accent! I'd been swindled.

Now, it's one thing to be cheated on a $10 CD but quite another to lose thousands of dollars. Our nutconomy is structured in such a way that we squirrels don't see how we're being cheated of a part of our nuts. Someone who had a million dollars nine years ago would've lost 35% or $350,000 of their wealth due to the dollar's loss of value (caused by the Fed and government spending of course).

I repeatedly stress the need to understand how government affects our nutconomy because it can affect our lives in ways we might not see. Unless we understand what it's doing, we can't protect our store of nuts. We must, therefore, understand the real value of money and what government does to it. *We must know the real nature of money.* We must know the original nature and purpose of money in order to avoid being cheated.

After all, the reason I had a nagging suspicion I was hoodwinked on that *Thriller* album was because I knew what the original album sounded like. I knew M.J. never made a "Puerto Rico Unplugged" CD.

Warned Since 1776

As I said, *we must learn capital management to preserve, protect and compound our seed money (principal) so that the passive income we generate from it can grow beyond what's needed to pay for our living expenses.* The bigger the fruit tree, the more fruit it will yield. We can never be financially free unless our living expenses are less than the passive income we earn from our assets.

But we run into a huge problem in our quest for financial freedom: The value of the money we use to buy the assets that create the passive income which buys our time freedom, *depreciates*. And if our money is worth less, so is our passive income since it's also paid to us in money.

The process of compounding interest is slowed down or even reversed if we don't do anything about the dollar's devaluation. In the example above, I said if we held $1 million in cash for the past eight or nine years, you would have lost $350,000 in value.

Q: Where does the value go? A: It's spent by the government.

How the government does this is best described by the father of economics, Adam Smith, in his book, *The Wealth of Nations* (first published in 1776):

For in every country of the world, I believe, the avarice and injustice of princes and sovereign states, abusing the confidence of their subjects, have by degrees diminished the real quantity of metal, which had been originally contained in their coins. The Roman As, in the latter ages of the Republic, was reduced to the twenty-fourth part of its original value, and, instead of weighing a pound, came to weigh only half an ounce. The English pound and penny contain at present about a third only; the Scots pound and penny about a thirty-sixth; and the French pound and penny about a sixty-sixth part of their original value. By means of those operations the princes and sovereign states which performed them were enabled, in appearance, to pay their debts and to fulfill their engagements with a smaller quantity of silver than would otherwise have been requisite. It was indeed in appearance only; for their creditors were really defrauded of a part of what was due to them. All other debtors in the state were allowed the same privilege, and might pay with the same nominal sum of the new and debased coin whatever they had borrowed in the old. Such operations, therefore, have always proved favourable to the debtor, and ruinous to the creditor, and have sometimes produced a greater and more universal revolution in the fortunes of private persons, than could have been occasioned by a very great public calamity (Ch. 4).

Did you pick up what he was putting down?

In case you didn't, historians have recently uncovered a long lost letter Smith had written to Thomas Jefferson about money. Because he wasn't writing the letter for publication purposes, he was very informal in his use of language:

Man, I heard ya'll thinkin bout insurrectin against his royal pomp and circumstance King George. Yo, I knew what *that* was about—you Americans don't like nobody foolin with ya'lls money. I don't blame you though, despite what people be thinkin, I know it aint just about no tax on some tea. Shoot, I'm an economist, I know this is some real stuff, some real economics are involved.

Look, no one likes it when people be playin with their money. But you know what? King Georgy got another way to get that money man. Let me break it down to ya by tellin you a story of what happened to me the other day that just ticked me off man.

Well, you know how I like to look good right? That's just how I roll. So I took my wig down to that shop WigPro on 116th and Vine to get it patched up. I drop it off and tell the dude, "I'll catch ya later."

I return a few hours later and you wouldn't *believe* what this fool was tryin to do. Man, he had the nerve to try and give me back a wig that had less hair than the one I dropped off! This fool was out of his *mind*! I was like, "Yo, I didn't leave my wig up in here with a bald spot in it. Why you tryin to hussle me man? Just give me back my full wig!"

But you know what T? That had me thinkin about you boys in America. Ya'll need to make sure ya'll use money that can't be counterfeited by the government. Governments always be tryin to pull one over on you. Just like that fool at WigPro, they can take a full head of Wig and try to give you back an old one with hardly any hair in it.

Governments always be doin that. You know these fools have been diluting money since days of Caesar? Towards the last days of Rome, their money called the As was only worth like 24% of its original value. That's not all though...it used to weigh like a pound but in the end, it weighed half an ounce!

Ain't nothin changed though T, ain't nothing changed. I was complainin bout how expensive everything was in my hood cause our pound is only worth like 30% of what it used to. But then I went over to my aunt's castle up in Scotland and you know what? Their pound be only worth like 36% of what it used to be. I also got a letter from my buddy Pierre up in France and he tells me their money only be worth 66% of what it used to.

But you know why them princes be doin this right? Cuz they can buy all the bling they want on credit man. They're ballin out of control T. You should see the diamonds—the rocks they be given their ladies. And you know what they do when they gotta pay they creditors? They just melt down the gold they got, put some crap in it as a filler and give the unsuspectin lender less money back without their knowledge. That ain't right.

Look T, I'm a smart dude and all I gotta say is this: ya'll better make sure that future generations of your peeps be havin some kind of money these princes can't counterfeit. Even if you use gold, you'll need to use ridges around coins to keep people from dilutin it. Good luck!

P.S., Hey T, word on the street is that you…uhmm…how do I say this? Let's just say that I heard you acquired a taste for darker berries. Is that true? Hit me back.

Your boy,

--A. Smith.

Okay so I forged the letter. You got me.

I wanted to do so because we've somehow forgotten how crucial an understanding of money is to understanding economic activity. Investors usually think about types of assets like stocks, bonds, real estate but usually forget to think about money itself (currency). We should consider it as an investment.

The starting point of investing should be an understanding how different types of currencies affect our financial goals. Millions of people want to buy their time freedom by being financially free; the sooner they understand the true nature and use of money, the sooner they'll achieve it. Saving wisely, as you'll see, is not just about quantity, it's also about quality.

"Most of our assumptions have outlived their uselessness." ~Marshall McLuhan.

Why We Need Money

To understand money, we must start with the basics because it's so important in understanding everything else. A first question to ask is, "Why do we need money?" What is its purpose? A: Since all commerce is based on a trade, money just makes trading easier.

Imagine how difficult business would be *without* money. Let's say you grew wheat for a living. In order to buy other things like milk, you'd have to trade wheat directly for it. You'd have to pack your truck and aimlessly drive around trying to find that *one* dairy farmer who needs wheat.

The first farmer you meet doesn't need wheat. A second dairy farmer only buys organic wheat at his local Whole Foods Market. A third farmer has a wheat allergy! What do you do?

If you had *money*, you could buy the milk you needed and sell your wheat to someone else later. Money is, then, just a 'medium of exchange'.

In order to make trading possible, money had to have value *in itself*. Before the days of a paper money dictatorship, gold was seen by free people everywhere as that thing that had this intrinsic value.

People didn't have to worry about whether the fisherman, rancher or dairy farmer would find value in the gold coins that they were offering in trade. People have always valued gold.

"Money was never a big motivation for me, except as a way to keep score. The real excitement is playing the game." ~Donald Trump

Cortez Loved the Bling Bling

Gold *spontaneously* became money because everyone thought it was valuable. It was natural to use gold as money; that's why economists refer to gold as *natural money*.

No government had to force people to accept gold. People throughout history have been willing to risk their lives for gold. All the explorers we learned about in history class were driven by a desire to find their pot of gold.

Here's what the great Adam Smith had to say about their motives:

1. They wanted the bling: *"Nothing less precious than gold seemed worthy of their attention."*
2. They all wanted the bling: *"All the other enterprises of the Spaniards in the new world . . . seem to have been prompted by the same motive."*
3. They looked everywhere for bling: *"It was the sacred thirst of gold that carried Oieda, Nicuessa, and Vasco Nugnes de Bablo, to the isthmus of Darien, that carried Cortez to Mexico, and Almagro and Pizzarro to Chile and Peru, [Antonio Banderas to Los Angeles and Aunt Jemima to North Carolina].*
4. Is there any bling in the house?: *"When those adventurers arrived upon any unknown coast, their first enquiry was always if there was any gold to be*

found there; and according to the information they received concerning this particular, they determined either to quit the country or settle it."[3]

I love this historical account because it shows just how much people naturally valued gold. The first question explorers would ask when arriving at a new land was whether there was gold there, if not, they'd split.

"A strong passion for any object will ensure success, for the desire of the end will point out the means." ~Henry Hazlitt.

The Dollar

Technically speaking, the dollar is not money because paper has no value.

So why do we use paper money? We use it because we're forced to.

Why *force* people to accept paper money anyway? Doesn't that peak your curiosity? Why would the government make the use of any *other* currency illegal if people want to use it? Don't we live in a free market system? If you can choose who you do business with, you should be able to choose the money you accept in trade.

One reason is this: If people had a *choice*, they wouldn't necessarily use the dollar. They'd choose to use something that held value. They'd choose something not just backed by "the full faith" of our government. Over centuries, different civilizations have used different things like silver, copper, salt and gold as money—but never paper.

A second reason to force citizens to use *only* the dollar is to make confiscating the public's wealth much easier for the government. If they try to counterfeit money and people had a choice of currency, they would just start using that other currency. And if the government tried to counterfeit that new currency by printing it, then the market will pick yet another currency and so on. You can't pin citizens down to one currency and dilute it without force.

Adam Smith pointed out that when governments skim off the top, they're "abusing the confidence of their subjects." That's because the squirrels in the olden days had no idea their nuts were being counterfeited. For the most part, most people today have no idea that it's happening even though more information is available about how the monetary system works. And the ones that understand monetary policy are beginning to understand that the

---

[3] The Wealth of Nations, Chapter 7, Part One

government may never stop printing money to pay for its expenses. At this point, the most important difference between gold and paper money can be made clear.

If you think about it, it's *weird* for people to exclusively use one currency that its government has complete control of. Think about how risky that is for a moment.

You could wake up broke because other people have lost confidence in the dollars you hold in your pocket. We either trust politicians or we trust in gold, there's no middle ground. So far, the market has trusted the government's handling of our nation's wealth. But more and more investors are becoming frightened about our national debt. If enough people realize our government has no intention of stopping the massive printing of money, the dollar could become worthless overnight.

Investors don't understand that the U.S. is caught in a debt trap just yet. Our financial risk is that enough investors find out we are stuck in such a trap.

If money isn't backed by a thing of real value, we're at the mercy of other people's perception of what they think the dollar is worth, that thing in our pocket we've worked so hard to get. *Money is supposed to be a store of value.* That's what makes us agree to give up our time for it. When a retiree thinks of her retirement fund, she should see it as a reflection of the value she's provided to society during her working years. It's been *earned*.

But because the value of paper money is *elastic*, the government can step in and ask, "Has it really been earned? Just because you're retired doesn't mean we can't tax the pay you earned 20 years ago."

Government is the only power that can erase the value of the work we've *already* put it. And it has the power to erase the *entire* value we've created through decades of hard work. The collapse of the value of the dollar is a possibility.

Right now, the dollar's value is hanging by a thread. All that's required for its collapse is some catalyst, a trigger. Napoleon once said there's "a thin line between the sublime and the ridiculous". We've recently seen this to be true. We woke up one day and Greece's debt problems (an economy the size of large U.S. city) caused a worldwide selloff and a large drop in the Euro's value.

In May of 2010, the stock market dropped a thousand points in a single day because of a computer glitch but three months later, the market hadn't fully recovered. Holding on to cash is therefore a very risky proposition in many

133

different ways when compared with gold—something all people everywhere have always valued.

"If you were to stash away a shoebox of money for 5 years, would you choose to fill it with gold or with dollars?" ~Ron Paul.

Invention of Paper Money

If you recall the chart of gold prices from an earlier letter, from 2000 to 2010, gold appreciated more than any other investment class.

From 2001, the price of gold has gone up by 400%. If your dollars were backed by gold, they would have *also* appreciated by 400%. So the cost of everything in the economy would be 400% cheaper due to the dollar's increased value.

Think of what this means for people living through this recession. Imagine how far unemployment benefits would go if healthcare, gas, education and food were 400% cheaper. Health insurance premiums would be $37/month on average and gas would be $0.70 cents/gallon.

It's not always easy to explain how our paper money makes us poorer, but it should be obvious by now that *we've made the worst trade in the history of mankind* by using paper money not backed by something of real *value*. So why do we have paper money if it has so many obvious drawbacks?

Reason One: *Paper money was invented to allow governments to finance wars.* All wars have been financed by debt because it's extremely costly. During the American Revolution, Congress created the Continental to finance its war with England. During the Civil War, Congress went off gold and issued Greenbacks to finance its war with the South. To fight the Vietnam War, we printed a huge amount of money.

But why print paper to fund war anyway? Why not just raise taxes?

Well, because if we had to pay for wars upfront, we'd only fight the necessary ones—defensive wars (an inconvenience for the State).

Reason Two: *Paper money allows corporations to get cheap credit.* Money is like every other product in the marketplace. If there's too much of it, it becomes less valuable (cost of borrowing goes down). If there's less of it around, it becomes more valuable (cost of borrowing goes up).

So when wealthy industrialists urged Congress to create the Federal Reserve System, they were really interested in reducing their borrowing costs by making credit more available. But what's made cheap for some in an economy is always made more expensive for others.

The Central Builder

Here's how it works. Imagine if all the renters in Los Angeles decided they wanted to reduce their rents. And in order to do so, they convinced Congress to fund the building of two million apartment buildings. The cost of rent would fall by 80 or 90% due to the two million new apartment buildings.

That's how we should understand the cost of money (interest). We rent money. When anything in the marketplace, such as renting money, is cheap for *one* group of people, it is expensive for *another*. So, if our central bank makes the cost of borrowing money cheap for corporations, it makes it expensive for others.

If renters in Los Angeles get to rent apartments at a low price because a *Central Builder* build millions of new units over night (printing money), who pays the cost? Obviously anyone who owned rental units in Los Angeles before the new units flooded the market would see the value of their holdings destroyed.

In the same way, people who own dollars before the new money floods the economy will see the value of their dollars *or any dollar denominated assets they own*, fall. As Adam Smith said, printing money is "favorable to the debtor [the government and corporations], and ruinous to the creditor."

So who are the creditors that are ruined by the massive printing of dollars? They are the taxpayers. Anyone who uses dollars or saves dollars or owns assets that are denominated in dollars are defrauded.

You now understand quite a bit about how the American economy works. And this understanding helps us understand other aspects of our economic world a little better:

1. You can see why the government would force everyone to use just one currency—it is the only way to tax our money. And knowing what they're up to can inform you to counteract their scheme.
2. It also makes it easier to explain the growing wealth divide in America. Every year, wealth is being transferred to the richest few at the top who get their hands on the new money (newly printed money) first. Those who get their hands on the new money first profit at the expense of people at the bottom of the ladder. They get the bread fresh out of the oven, before it dries out. They use the new money before the inflation eats away at its value.

3. It's easier to understand why inflation is so much more devastating for the poor, lower class and the elderly. These people earn so very little, it's much more difficult for them to save, invest and get out of a cyclical hand to mouth existence. The Fed's confiscation of their money's value is an enormous cost for them because they have so few dollars to begin with.

4. If the father of economics says that the counterfeiting of money has "sometimes produced a greater and more universal revolution [loss of value] in the fortunes of private persons, than could have been occasioned by a very great public calamity", maybe it's important to understand that money, rather than bringing us economic salvation or prosperity, can utterly ruin our national wealth.

We're going into detail about the nature of money because the point of capital management is to preserve and grow your principal, to use it to create passive income that's greater than living costs. Now, here's the third reason we use paper as money.

Reason Three: *Paper money was introduced to increase bank profits.* This should be obvious. After all, it was a group of bankers that drafted the legislation to establish the Federal Reserve in the first place. Banks always want to increase the amount of money they lend. The more they lend the more interest they can earn. The more debt there is in the economy, the more money banks make. It should be obvious that banks always want to *inflate* the money supply. To find out more about this, log onto Youtube.com and watch a documentary titled, *"Money, Banking and the Federal Reserve."*

Reason Four: *Paper money was invented to make paying for expensive government promises (entitlement programs) like Social Security much more manageable.* It also allows politicians to create new promises without having to pay for old ones.

Like the princes in Adam Smith's account above, government can borrow money from people enrolled in the Social Security program and when payment is due, melt down the gold (print money), add fillers and hand it back to the creditors. The creditors are the retirees who were suckered into paying 12.4% of their wages into this massive government scheme.

"A government that robs Peter to pay Paul can always depend on the support of Paul."
~George Bernard Shaw

Inflation is Confiscation

The word *inflation* should be changed to *confisflation* because it's plainly confiscatory.

I strongly warn against inflation because most people don't see how it eats away at savings and their ability to gain financial freedom. In a truly capitalistic society, all prices would go down year over year as entrepreneurs invest in more and more efficient ways of getting products to the market. The reason most prices rise every year is due to our government's inflation tax.

Although the inflation tax eats away *at least* 7% of our wealth every year, most investment advisors don't stress this point to their clients. A 7% tax is incredibly expensive when you compound the effects over a number of years. Investors who own stock in U.S. companies that earn their profits in dollars lose tens of thousands (if not more depending on the amount and length of their investment) as a result.

That the government is using the Fed to silently defraud taxpayers is obvious to see in their reporting of inflation numbers. To justify printing more money, our government fudges the numbers. When they report the inflation tax numbers, they don't include price increases in food or energy as part of their calculations.

When I explained this to a fellow squirrel over Hazelnut coffee, she exclaimed, "What? But those are the two biggest expenses for most squirrels!" For the middle class, retirees and the poor, food and energy costs make up a high percentage of their expenses. Obviously, their suffering, pain and financial worry are not a consideration for the Fed.

Their official excuse for not counting food and energy in their numbers is because the price of food and energy, they say, are volatile. Well, then why not use a 12 month average?

"Inflation is taxation without legislation." ~Milton Friedman

False Profits/High Taxes

One of the ways government *confisflates* private wealth is by taxing *false* profits. It might not do this intentionally but the result is the same. They create the economic conditions that enables them to tax false profits. It taxes false profits *by not allowing people to deduct the inflation tax when they file their returns.* Every year, all tax filers overestimate their incomes by the rate of inflation (7-9%).

137

During economic booms, *confisflation* is a big problem because individuals and companies report much higher earnings. In such times, squirrel spending is up, tree real estate prices go up, nut prices soar, squillionaires are created and everything is going through the roof. But all this wealth is a mirage, fake, phony.

But the federal government doesn't treat it as fake wealth. It still taxes people as if they'd really made higher wages and profits. It doesn't give the money back when the bubble economy they've created bursts.

Here's how this works on the local level. State and county governments also over tax people during credit created economic bubbles. In California, for example, everyone is taxed a percentage of their home's value, usually around 1%.

Now if property prices are inflated, local governments can collect more tax revenue than they would have if prices remained closer to their real values. But now that prices have come back down, the millions that homeowners overpaid in property taxes won't be refunded. At the very least, homeowners now know enough to register lower home values to save money.

We should always be sure to save in a hundred different ways if we expect to remain get rich; these are just some of the more unseen ways money leaks through our pockets. The only people who experience capital loss are those who don't put in the time to become educated about economics. We're never trapped. Education *always* gives us options and leverage.

Your Loving Uncle,
    Akinaw.

Two Global Trends
You Can't Ignore

Dear Kidus,

I've given you all the bad news about paper money because the dangers of misunderstanding it are great. More importantly, if we understand money clearly, other parts of the nutconomy will easily be understood. Here's a list of the negative impacts of money depreciation we've previously outlined:

1. Increases our living expenses and, therefore, reduces the amount of money we've got to invest.
2. Increases our tax liability because we can't deduct inflation from our earnings. Inflation reduces the real value of our wages.
3. Reduces the real value of our assets.
4. Reduces the value of our passive income.
5. Paper money exposes every citizen living in a debt burdened economy to the possibility of a currency collapse.

Now here's the good news: We live in a global economy in which we've got all sorts of choices, including the currency we choose to hold our money in.

Our money doesn't have to be trapped in a single economy. The way to escape the inflation tax is by investing in foreign economies with appreciating currencies.

Since the values of different currencies rise and fall relative to all the rest, so does the comparative wealth of different economies. For example, since our wealth is measured in dollars, and it falls 20% against Germany's currency (the Euro), the net worth of Squirrelmericans (*everything* in our economy) also falls by 20%. Germans would then be 20% richer than American citizens.

It's this nutconomic understanding we ought to use to make our investment decisions. Here's how I see it. We've got two things that are occurring and must occur in the global marketplace.

1. Foreign currencies must appreciate against the dollar: As foreign economies grow, their currencies grow because its value is tied to the strength of their economic output. As capitalism spreads across

the globe like a flood, foreign economies will be growing at a much faster pace. It's an opportunity to grow our net worth alongside them.

2. The U.S. dollar will depreciate for two reasons. First, because politicians don't have the courage to decrease spending or increase taxes, more and more of our budget will be financed by debt. Secondly, we're a developed economy with no chance of reaching double digit growth rates.

In either case, we have two guarantees: our money can appreciate or depreciate. Your money can appreciate if it's invested in fast growing foreign economies or, it can depreciate in the States.

Let's assume we invest a greater portion of our income in foreign economies. If we do so, the four of the five negative consequences of the dollar's depreciation (listed above) will be eliminated:

1. Decreases our living expenses. Since our money will be appreciating against the dollar, our costs at home will be kept low. Remember that costs only go up if the value of our money goes down. Congress can't print foreign currencies.

2. Increases the value of our assets. Imagine you own a nice loft in Brazil that's appreciated 10% in a single year. Now, let's say you sold it to take a 10% profit. But we also get a bonus if Brazil's currency (the Real) has appreciated against the dollar. When proceeds of the sale are converted, you get more dollars per Real.

3. In the same way, our passive income (rents, dividends, interest, etc) paid in foreign currencies will also appreciate.

4. And lastly, the biggest benefit of investing in foreign economies: You avoid the possible complete collapse of the U.S. dollar.

Of course, I don't want any of this to come true. I want what's best for the U.S. because I love just about everything about it. Maybe if enough people understand economics, a collapse can be averted. I remain hopeful because America has always come out on top.

Your Loving Uncle,
    Akinaw.

Understanding How Government Scams Taxpayers

Dear Kidus,

There's a reason saving capital has taken such a prominent place in my letters.

Do you remember what happened to the Squirrelmericans in our story? They went hungry and cold for only one reason—they ate up their store of nuts. At the same time, they weren't planting new nut trees. What else could cause squirrels to experience hunger?

The answer to our nutconomic problems is simple—we waste nuts (capital) on a massive scale because we don't understand what it is or why it's important. The only way to replace wasted nuts is to economize/save more nuts as we go forward. We can't bring wasted nuts back to the forest trees by printing nutty money; we can only do so by planting new nut trees.

What most voters don't understand is *how* the overconsumption of capital happens. There are three ways that capital is wasted:

1. The Fed, as we've seen, is a huge factor in getting people to overspend by tricking them into thinking they've got more nuts than they do. A false sense of financial security creates problems for the whole forest because it leads most squirrels to eat their food before the winter sets in. One financial commentator put it best: "Americans were consuming their capital without knowing it." The Fed creates the "not knowingness" that leads to capital waste. Review the letters on economic literacy to understand this further.

2. A second way in which capital is destroyed is through war spending. With over 900 bases in 140 nations worldwide, the total U.S. military budget accounts for 50 to 60% of the world's total military budget. Big military budgets are especially wasteful *in an age of global capitalism* because it's a consumer of capital and wealth—not a creator of it.

3. A third way we waste capital is through welfare spending (corporate and public). Welfare spending is also mostly unproductive but unlike military spending, its only saving grace is that the money we spend on those programs at least stays in our system as recipients spend it. It's recycled.

Both sides (warfare and welfare) contribute to the inefficiency of the total system by increasing taxes to pay for things that give us less happiness. What Squirrelmerica needs is a new nut party whose only purpose is to preserve capital.

The Social Security Scam

Every government welfare program is wasteful by *necessity*. Part of the reason my heart goes out to the lower classes is because almost every government program or department promises economic salvation but eventually ends up impoverishing them.

Social Security is both spiritually and economically impoverishing: The program is premised on the idea that government can take better care of you than you can for yourself. The program is economically impoverishing because the people who pay into the system will *never* get the same amount of money back out. Even if they seem to be getting a corresponding amount back, it's an illusion because it will be paid for by a devaluation of the value of the benefits—through the inflation tax.

People who live off dividends don't have to pay 12.4% of their incomes into the Social Security System. But if you're a wage earner, you *cannot* get around this tax.

"The more you seek security, the less of it you have. But the more you seek opportunity, the more likely it is that you will achieve the security that you desire." ~Brian Tracy.

Let's Do the Shuffle

Social Security is called a "pay-as-you-go" system—as you work, the government takes your money and gives it to other Social Security recipients. To get you to participate in the system, the government promises to deduct pay from other people's wages and give it to you when you stop working.

Because it's set up like a real Ponzi scheme, it can work as long as there are more payers than recipients. When the program started, the worker to beneficiary ratio was about 16 to 1. This means that because there were so many more payers than recipients, the government should have an enormous surplus. Even with retirees living much longer, there are still about 3 workers for every 1 beneficiary. The resulting surplus in 2008 was $180 billion.

If the Social Security Fund had a surplus of $180 billion when the worker to beneficiary ratio was a measly 3 to 1, it should've had much more when the worker to beneficiary ratio was 16 to 1. And it did. Since 1982, Social Security has run a *surplus* of over $2.5 trillion. So why then, is it broke? As Snoop Dogg would ask, "Where all them greenbacks at?"

The answer is that the government "borrowed it" and spent it on other programs without having any way of paying it back. It's called an "intra-governmental debt." Bernie Madoff would have called it "intra-investmental debt."

Whenever the government takes money out of the fund to spend it elsewhere, it writes an I.O.U. to the fund. So that $180 billion "surplus" in 2008 is actually an I.O.U. So, in effect, the Treasury owes itself money.

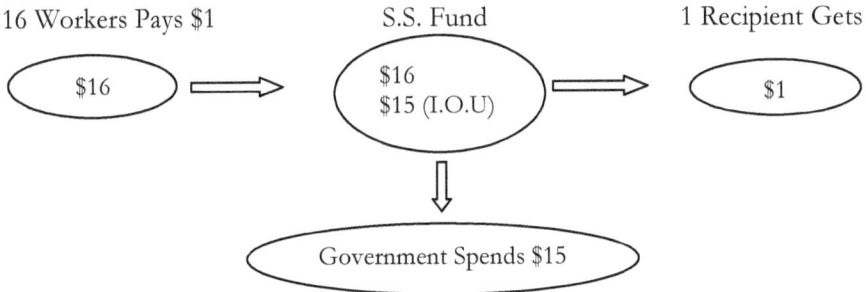

The Effect

This means that whenever you pay 12.4% of your income into the Social Security fund, each dollar paid creates a dollar of debt *plus* an interest liability for new people joining the system. By 2017, the total debt liability will be about $3.5 trillion.

That $3.5 trillion figure *must* be collected in the future through taxes. After all, the money is owed to people who would've paid into the system.

If you're following the story so far, Squerrelmericans trusted their Squirreliticians to safeguard their nuts so they'll have some left when their furs are thin and grey. Of all the places Squirrelmericans can invest 12.4% of their incomes, they're forced, *by law*, to invest in Acorn Treasury notes that earn a negative return.

But here's a twist to the story. The negative return isn't incurred only by people who are entering the system but also *workers who are already receiving benefits*. In both cases, when government borrows from the Social Security fund at interest, we must not forget they've got only one way of paying it back—by raising taxes. Those taxes fall on everyone—people in the system (workers) and retirees.

"Collecting more taxes than is absolutely necessary is legalized robbery." ~Calvin Coolidge.

Filling in the Gap

The government has two tax options: (a) increase taxes/print money (same thing); (b) borrow money. If they choose to borrow money to keep the system solvent, by 2082, the Social Security fund's *deficit* will reach $30 to $40 trillion and they'll just create a bigger hole. And by the way, we'll have solved nothing in the process. We'd only create a problem that's ten times as big as the initial $3.5 trillion gap. The government's most likely option is to pick option C: "All the evils above."

In the past, the government has resorted to increasing the Social Security tax in order to keep this Ponzi scheme going. In 1950, the Social Security tax was 3%, then moved up to 6% in 1960, 8.4% in 1970 and finally reached 12.4% in 2008. We have all the reason in the world to believe these continual tax increases on the worker will continue into the future. That they have no problem printing money should also be obvious from our recent history.

"If we become increasingly humble about how little we know, we may be more eager to search."
~John Templeton.

What This Means for Workers

There's a reason Social Security creates a net negative return for recipients. If inflation is really 6 to 9%, but the government indexes your payments to a phony 3% rate (which is a tax to begin with), you're being cheated of a big portion of your Social Security benefits.

144

The myth put out by the government is that Social Security payments are indexed for inflation. Well, it works great if you can pay for inflation and *have the exclusive power to determine the rate of inflation.* Obviously, ponzi schemer, Bernie Madoff would see how extremely convenient it must be for the government to referee its own game.

As government continues to print money to pay for its deficits, the value of Social Security benefits will be greatly diminished because recipients are paid in dollars. In addition to entitlement programs, just the federal budget deficit alone will get up to $23 trillion according to figures released by the Obama administration.

As the government uses inflation to manage its Ponzi scheme, Social Security recipients won't be able to keep up with rising costs.

"God grants liberty only to those who love it, and are always ready to guard and defend it."
~Daniel Webster.

Should've Would've Could've

Think about how much more we can all have if we invested 12.4% of our incomes into emerging market economies every year for the next 20 years instead of U.S. Treasuries. Instead of trading 12.4% of our wages for higher taxes in the future, we could earn 200 to 400% in the next 10 years if we were free to do so. Here are some recent facts (2003 until 2009) that indicate what workers are missing out on by not having the opportunity to invest in emerging markets:

1. Since 2003, Brazil's *currency alone* has appreciated 80%.
2. Since 2000, India's stock market has returned 136%.
3. Brazil has returned 314%.
4. Russia has returned 689%.
5. China has returned 100%.

This kind of "once in a lifetime" growth story is what wage workers won't be able to see. This is how most welfare schemes always end—by destroying the livelihoods of the very people it seeks to help.

"If you do not expect the unexpected you will not find it." ~Heraclitus.

The Workaround

Obviously, where there's a will, there's a way. Workers must take things into their own hands since the government is not really restricted by a constitution anymore—they can do what they want. My recommendation is the following:

1. If you must work as a wage or a salaried employee, do so as little as possible. Your goal should be to live off of capital gains, dividends and interest. In that way, you won't have to pay social security taxes. You save an automatic 12.4% per year you'll be able to invest for a positive return.
2. Barter as much as possible and invest the taxes you would've paid into emerging markets.
3. Become a minister—they don't have to pay into the system.
4. Reduce your expenses as much as you can. Downsize or move out to the suburbs to save money on housing. With the advent of the internet, you can do business anywhere.
5. Your goal is to cash flow in as many ways as possible. But you can't expect to do that in an economy that's both wasteful and burdened with debt. Emerging markets are a path to economic salvation for various reasons but one the biggest is that there's so much opportunity in these places, companies are even offering double digit dividend yields.
6. Some people should consider retiring early in order to exchange their dollars for foreign currencies while the dollar has some value left. Retiring or living abroad on the cheap is coming to an end for Americans.
7. I know this one sounds extreme: Young people should consider renouncing their citizenship and working abroad where opportunities exist. It's not extreme when we consider that young people are inheriting $108 trillion of debt. Anyway, Western trained people are in demand in these emerging economies. Moving your citizenship and your money may be impossible to do in the future. Our government is taking steps to close that door (or at least, make it very expensive to do so).
    a. The U.S. is the only industrialized nation that taxes the earnings of its citizens living abroad. If you're an American working in Brazil, you must pay taxes twice (in Brazil and the

U.S.). To avoid this double taxation, many expatriates have been forced to renounce their citizenship. There has recently been a big spike in the number of American citizens renouncing their citizenships.

b. In 2008 Congress passed the HEART ACT which made changes to expatriate taxation, making it harder for Americans to renounce their citizenship and protect their assets if the American empire begins to crumble. Under the new tax rules, if your income in the last five years was over $124,000 or your net worth is more than $2 million, you'll be liable to pay income on all foreign income earned for 10 years after you've renounced your citizenship!

But let's imagine you get to renounce your citizenship without a tax penalty. You'll still need a good tax attorney to plan your visits to the U.S. If you come back to the U.S. and stay for at least 30 days, you'll once again be taxed on your worldwide income.

The part that most upsets me is if an expatriate comes back to visit a friend, intending to leave before the 30 day tax trap, and happens to die on day 15, all of his or her worldwide estate will be taxed by the U.S. government.

Remember that to guard your capital is to guard your financial freedom. You must always understand how your economic and political system is structured in order to protect what you've earned. It's only through awareness that we either compound our financial successes or failures.

Your Loving Uncle,
    Akinaw.

Quigley's Prophecy: China Inc. vs. the U.S.

Dear Kidus,

One of the most interesting ways to understand the importance of capital management is to see how it plays out in the rise and fall of nations.

A Cosmic Transformation

It's amazing how fast things change in the world.

When I came to the U.S. in 1986, the Soviet Union was still a feared superpower, John Paul II was the Pope, the Euro and the European Union didn't exist, the national deficit was only at a couple trillion and America's economy had no direct competition. We didn't have eBay, Amazon.com, the internet, Brittany Spears, Beanie Babies and Michael Jackson was still black.

But in the short span of 20 years, the entire world *completely* changed. It feels like just yesterday I was sporting braces and jamming to Boys II Men on my Sony Walkman.

We wake up the next day and billions of people have been integrated into the capitalist world after being released from the iron grip of communism. And strangely enough, the one noteworthy Communist state left has become the world's best capitalist. In those same 20 years, the United States, once the world's biggest creditor, became the biggest debtor.

Who would've thought China would be America's *creditor*? How did the world get turned upside down almost overnight? It has been turned upside down in subtle ways that the man on the street may not understand. We don't understand what's happened because we underestimate the importance of capital as a weapon in global politics.

Squirrelmericans don't understand the incredible power the Chinese have over the United States. Other nations are able to influence our foreign policy because we're indebted to them.

"The rich rule over the poor, and the borrower is servant to the lender."~Proverbs 22:7.

The Hidden Danger of Debt

I've never had anything positive to say about our national debt.

Politicians, I'm afraid, may not understand the role debt plays in destroying empires. After a certain amount of debt's been incurred by *any* state, it takes a small trigger or catalyst to push its economy into an abyss.

It's been said, for example, that Ronald Reagan used debt to push the Soviet Union into bankruptcy. Reagan, seeing the economic weakness of the Soviet Union, dragged them into an expensive military spending contest because he knew they couldn't keep up. Now, if Reagan proved huge military budgets can bankrupt empires, maybe Squirrelmerica can learn from his experiment.

Regardless of how it's created, debt is always the "straw that breaks the camel's back." If we keep adding endless amounts of debt to our national ledger, we may wake up to find the entire system has cratered under that weight. We never know when that day of reckoning will be.

Let me illustrate the hidden danger of debt through a story I saw on the news. On July 1st 2009, 911 emergency responders in Sumter County, Florida got a call from a sobbing dad. "She got out of the cage last night and got into the baby's crib and strangled her to death," he cried.

When police and paramedics showed up at the house, they found a dead 2 year old girl that had been strangled to death by a pet Burmese python. The python and a second snake were kept in the house. It had somehow gotten out of its cage the night before, silently slithered into the baby's room, slid into the crib and crushed the little girl to death.[4]

Every night the little girl was put to bed, tragedy was just around the corner—the snake was just down the hall. But the danger was unrecognized for two reasons. According to Fish and Wildlife Conservation spokeswoman, Joy Hill, no Floridian had ever been killed by a non-venomous snake. But it still happened. Another factor that made the tragedy so unlikely was that the snake was probably well fed. But the tragedy still occurred.

Our federal debt, like the python, is always on the verge of breaking out of its cage and destroying the prosperity of current and future generations of Americans.

Some people may object to such a comparison. "How can you compare something as sterile as debt with a heartbreaking story of a toddler being strangled to death?"

---

[4] http://www.foxnews.com/story/0,2933,529835,00.html

But we must remember that it was something as lifeless as a German currency crisis which paved the way for Hitler to assume power. This led, in turn, to the deaths of fifty million people.

It was our Federal Reserve Bank's irresponsible actions that caused flesh and blood to jump out of New York skyscrapers during the Great Depression. And more recently, as an indirect result of the Fed's same money policies, a very desperate, angry man flew his single engine plane into an IRS building in Texas.

One of the scariest aspects of human behavior is a complete lack of *causal* thinking. The temptation is always to think, "Well, that can't happen here." My point is, "Yes it can…it can always happen." Germany was one of the most cultured civilizations in Europe but the Nazis still rose to power. It was so cultured and advanced, in fact, it alone accounted for over a quarter of all Nobel Prize winners prior to the start of World War II.

People are not as alarmed as they ought to be about the hidden consequences of debt.

"Blessed are the young, for they shall inherit the national debt." ~Herbert Hoover.

The Debt Weapon

As I said, the Chinese are becoming much more powerful than we want to acknowledge. In some ways, we're at their mercy.

First, China or Big Daddy (as I like to call it) can cut off our credit card or reduce our credit limit. Consider the consequences. If the Chinese don't show up to buy more Treasury notes at our monthly "auction future generations into slavery" events, our fragile economy may collapse. It would collapse because our interest on borrowing money would *skyrocket* if Bid Daddy doesn't increase our credit limit; without access to more credit, our government would grind to a halt.

A simple announcement of a Chinese boycott of Treasury auctions would be enough to cause an economic crisis.

Secondly, China has another weapon they could use.

They could decide to dump the hundreds of billions of dollars of Treasuries they own, at which point, our entire economic system would collapse. Fear would drive people to dump the dollar and hyperinflation would follow. This threat wouldn't exist of course if, like the Chinese government, we had trillions of dollars of budget *surpluses.*

151

"Debt is the fatal disease of republics, the first thing and the mightiest to undermine governments and corrupt the people." ~Wendell Phillips.

New Definition of Power

How did it all happen so fast? We're watching a transformation in the structure of global power that's very fascinating. By far, the shift is going to be the biggest in recorded history. Why is it happening? Why is it happening so fast?

The shift in global power is taking place at an alarming pace because China has discovered what the famous historian Carroll Quigley has called "an instrument of expansion." It's a much more efficient way to expand and the Chinese have been using this secret weapon for awhile without our noticing.

China is using *capitalism* as their instrument of expansion; and interestingly enough, it's a weapon that gets bigger and bigger the more it's used. In other words, making money and compounding their economic growth is a far more efficient way to gain global power than war or making enemies. The more China saves and invests, the more it has, and the more it has, the more it can save and invest in itself.

We live in a much more competitive world. The nations which can attract the most capital will win the race for global power. Russia understands the importance of capital. Recently, Russian president Dimitry Medvedev urged his countrymen to abolish capital gains taxes on direct foreign capital investment. Russia is playing by the new rules of global capitalism. They tried the old path of global militarism and bankrupted themselves.

China learned from Russia's experience and they too were on the verge of social unrest when they decided to liberalize their economy. Since allowing direct foreign investment into its economy and freeing the private ambitions of its people to meet their own ends, they've grown at a rate of almost 10% per year. China is a Communist nation in name only. They don't have property taxes or the social safety nets like Social Security or Medicare that we have. That lack of a safety net encourages Chinese citizens to save, invest, and be productive.

Even though its citizens only have a yearly income of $3,600, they have more money saved up than any other economy in the world! Their high savings rate partly explains their sudden rise to power because they have more investable funds to expand their capitalistic empire. It's been said the pen is mightier than sword. In the next 100 years, we'll be saying, "Money is more powerful than the guns."

"Rather go to bed without dinner, than rise in debt." ~Benjamin Franklin.

How Empires Grow and Why They Fall

Every major empire has used some method to expand. In the days of the British Empire, a method Britain used to expand was its Navy's *absolute* power over international seas.

It was as much a force for expansion as it was a deterrent. The Royal Navy was, for example, the only thing that kept Napoleon, history's greatest general, off Britain's shores. Napoleon once said, "If I could master the English Channel for six hours, I would master the world." But he couldn't get across that channel.

The tool of expansion (Royal Navy) that worked to the advantage of the Brits in protecting their shores, didn't work for other purposes. Unfortunately for the Brits, they had to fight the American War of Independence on the ground, not on the sea. Their instrument of expansion didn't work on land.

The *process* by which the U.S. is slowly disintegrating was predicted by Carroll Quigley in his book, *"The Evolution of Civilizations"* (he also predicted the fall of the Soviet Union). He came up with his theory after studying 4,000 civilizations.

His theory was that whenever a civilization expands, it uses some method of expansion. *But*, that method ends up turning into the very thing that brings about its destruction once it becomes bureaucratized or institutionalized.

"Every revolution evaporates and leaves behind only the slime of a new bureaucracy."
~Franz Kafka

The Pre Civil War American South

Let's take a look at slavery as an example of this process. Before the Civil War, the American South used slavery to expand its power and influence. It worked for awhile but once they began to depend on slave labor, it became an institution. When that happened, they stopped coming up with new, more productive, efficient ways to produce agricultural output. They were, therefore, slowly digging their economic graves. Quigley says somewhere that industrial progress was "deplorable" in the South. So even without the Civil War, the

South would have eventually destroyed itself for *lack of imagination*, inventiveness.

"If everyone is thinking alike, then somebody isn't thinking." ~George S. Patton.

America's Rise and Fall (?)

In the same way, the U.S. has *institutionalized* its instrument of expansion—*capitalism*. I know what you're thinking: Isn't that what China's using? Yes, China is using capitalism, but it's doing so to expand, it hasn't become an institution yet. We no longer use capital to expand.

If we don't use capitalism to expand, we have a problem: If we eat up all our nuts, the forest's ecosystem will collapse. We must plant new trees but we're not doing it. So the thing that gave America its advantage is destroying it because it's being used for consumption purposes (through the institutions of welfare and warfare). It's as if we're falling on our own sword after we had used it to win the battle.

We see the *symptoms* of Quigley's prophecy in our economy. His *theory* predicted all the symptoms (and implications). That Professor Quigley's theory could've predicted that America would collapse under a burden of debt is *fascinating*.

How did he know we would stop becoming a producer nation and become a consumer nation? How did he know we'd come off of the gold standard in 1971 and in that way, remove the only barrier in fully turning America's instrument of expansion into an institution? How did he know we would expand social welfare year after year, even as our debt kept rising? How did he know that military spending would not be reduced even in peace times?

How did he know that George H. Bush (W's father) would get booted out of office for wanting to pay off the national debt? Papa Bush was an honest man but a bad politician because he didn't realize that spending had become an institution. Voters didn't want fiscal responsibility. How did Quigley know that the Federal Reserve would keep injecting credit into the economy in order to keep it from experiencing the pain of rebalancing? How did Quigley know that, as a result of all these actions, we would become a credit addicted economy?

Here's something that's even more fascinating: We're doing all this *unconsciously*. People on the left and on the right are in *complete* denial.

Quigley's predictions are also fascinating because he made them in 1961, a time when we had just become the most powerful nation on earth. We were an economic giant, producing products that shipped all over the world.

"A people that values its privileges above its principles soon loses both."
~Dwight D. Eisenhower.

China's Rise in the Age of Global Capitalism

The second alarming thing about China's rise is the advantage of building an empire without enemies. China has no ongoing sanctions against any country on earth. They also don't have a history of conflict with the world's 1.2 billion Muslims. Chinese companies have greater access to these huge, growing export markets that American companies can't compete in.

In Africa, the Chinese are shrewdly creating relationships and grabbing natural resources from the Nile to the tip of South Africa. In 2006, China invited the leaders of at least 50 African nations to Beijing to strengthen ties and make deals. The Chinese have loaned billions of dollars to help African nations build infrastructure—roads and bridges that must be built in order to transport natural resources to China and move their exports inland to one billion new customers.

In response to China's leadership role, African organizations are even hosting their events in Beijing. China has essentially monopolized influence in Africa.

But there's another way that China's influence in Africa affects America's interests. China will control a huge voting bloc in the U.N. by engaging these 50 African states in commerce (African nations represent about 25% of U.N. membership).

To give you an illustration of how entrenched China is in Africa, when I visited Ethiopia, all the roads in the capital were built by the Chinese. China's not just after natural resources—it's after one billion new customers. The day will come when we'll not be able to go anywhere in Africa without traveling on roads and bridges they've built to either transport natural resources out or move their exports inland.

"Do good to your friends to keep them, to your enemies to win them." ~Benjamin Franklin.

The Domino Effect Theory Revisited

Part of my thinking about global capitalism and why America is losing the battle for competitiveness is based on the domino theory of communism.

After World War II, as the West saw communism spreading, they slowly realized that if it wasn't contained, it would continue to spread from one nation to another—if one nation fell, another will follow (just like dominoes).

The same thing is happening in our world, except now, global capitalism is the thing that's spreading. China has adapted to this brave new world. *They're using capitalism as an instrument of expansion at the best possible time and we're using capitalism as an institution at the worst possible time.* This is very important to understand to get a clear picture of what the next 100 years will look like.

The *structure* of Squirrelmerican policies and thinking are better suited for a previous age, not for the capitalistic one to come. And as Quigley predicted, the U.S. may be unwilling to change its ways before it falls. Here are two pieces of evidence that prove his point:

1. **Welfare**. Instead of responsibly abolishing or reducing Medicare, Medicaid and Social Security costs, for example, every new administration creates larger and larger institutions that create more waste. Bush did this by passing a prescription drug bill that added *$8 trillion of new debt* (!) to a program that was already $15 to $20 trillion dollars in debt! Obama has also expanded the institution of welfare through the passage of the recent healthcare bill. Although the non-partisan Congressional Budget Office estimates that the new bill will save $143 billion from 2010 to 2019, 32 million people will now become dependent on government spending. The bill passed while allowing wasteful health insurers to maintain a legal monopoly.

2. **Warfare**. Recently, President Obama came out to call for a freeze on spending—on all federal spending "except the military" (our largest expense). Think about this: The U.S. accounts for over 50% of the world's total war budget. But communism is dead. We haven't had any noteworthy enemies since the Soviet Union fell. Why is it so large? Well, because it's become an institution. Special interests depend on war spending for money.

Both sides of the political spectrum are using spending as an *institution*.

However, despite the fact that 4,000 civilizations have risen and fallen, I still believe that if there is any culture that can self-correct, it is ours. There's just something special about America. Maybe its destiny is to be the only civilization that self-corrects before destroying itself.

Perhaps massive numbers of voters will learn that all of America's problems stem from the waste of capital. Maybe we can still beat Quigley's historical determinism.

Regardless of what happens in the future, I hope this little lesson in global capitalism helps you understand what the next 100 years may look like. More importantly, *I hope you understand the importance capital is playing in shifting global power. It was the accumulation of capital due to producing and saving that gave America such an edge in the world until it became a bureaucracy.*

In much the same way, it's the acquiring of capital through saving and production that's allowing the Chinese to expand so quickly across global.

"I can predict future happiness for Americans if they can prevent the government from wasting the labors of the people under the pretense of taking care of them." ~Thomas Jefferson.

Your Loving Uncle,
Akinaw.

Part IV

The Secrets of Productivity

How to Make Things

Dear Kidus,

Productivity should be one of the easiest concepts to understand about wealth consciousness. But even if it's simple to grasp, making the commitment to be productive isn't easy because of how Squirrelmerican society thinks about money.

St. Paul understood productivity when he said, "If a man will not work, he shall not eat." Now as simple as that sounds, the modern squirrel has done his best to bury that truth in the forest floor (the evidence is the huge debt burden that future generations will have to pay for). Modern economists have come up with ways to undermine the productive spirit. We're told that our economy depends on consumerism and that we can get along without a manufacturing base.

In the following letter, I'll show you that our biggest barrier to living a productive life is the thought forms we acquire from our society. Secondly, we'll pinpoint what it means to be productive and how to do it.

Don't Drink the Poison

Our entire political system is based on the idea that there's a way to get something for nothing. Some call for trickledown economics while others call for trickle up economics. But little trickles always lead to an ocean of debt. I call both plans economic violence. Our complicated legal tax code is proof that our society is always looking to get something at the expense of other taxpayers. *Participating in this way of thinking will have negative effects on your ability to be productive.*

"The state is that great fiction by which everyone tries to live at the expense of everyone else."
~Frederic Bastiat.

Don't Drink the Punch

In my college days, I learned a lot of things—including that professors shouldn't tell jokes. I remember one instance when a professor told joke that students thought was both a little crude and not that funny. It was a sociology

161

class and our professor decided to make things a bit interesting: "Why didn't Jim Jones make it as a comedian?" he asked. No response from the class.

"His punch line was too long!"

We all kind of shook our heads. He told the joke because we were talking about some disturbing issues in class that day. He said something else that disturbed me: We can never really escape the system completely. Like cult members who committed mass suicide by drinking poisoned punch, we also get in the punch line everyday to fill our cups. In other words, self-delusion is a human exercise. We rationalize our decisions. People need excuses to alleviate the guilt of knowing what they're doing is somehow wrong.

That explains a question I've found fascinating: "How has our culture come to believe that deficits don't matter?" Think about it. Say "deficits don't matter" slowly and listen to what you're saying. Maybe a good way to answer that question is to ask, "Who stands to lose something if the public didn't believe that mantra?"

At first, I suspected the "deficits don't matter" mantra was created for private hands to grab as much public money as possible through government spending before the public wakes to find out that deficits really *do* matter. But I don't think that's completely accurate.

The fact such a statement exists and works so well tells us something about the cleverness of politicians and political advisors but it also tells us something about the people who accept it. Propagandists know that there's a part of us all that wants to get something for nothing. But we'd feel guilty about stealing from future generations because we know it's wrong. So, they've created an alibi unproductive people were looking for to rationalize away the guilt. They coax us gently to accept the mantra so we don't have to feel bad about stealing (from our own children no less).

There's an implicit promise: "If you just accept this creed, you'll realize a benefit beside freedom from guilt—you'll get some of the new debt that others will have to pay for down the road."

If you take this bait, you will undermine your ability to be productive. You must assume total responsibility for getting what you want by making something the world wants. Business coach Brian Tracy has said that accepting total responsibility for every area of your life is the starting point of achievement. I agree.

Productivity starts with your mind and heart. It only has one prerequisite: Responsibility. You shouldn't believe that economic salvation comes from *without* because it comes from *within*. Refuse to participate in the get

162

something for nothing idea. Don't think that credit will bring you economic salvation. If you allow the greed and the economic violence of Squirrelmerica to affect your mind and heart, you cannot become a productive individual and your life's work will not last.

The American government is more than just wasteful, it's also spiritually corrosive. It corrupts the belief systems of its citizens because it sets the tone for our national identity. Emerson once said that "an institution is the extended shadow of one's soul". Programs like Social Security extend shadows of their own. Its existence requires that we accept a few ideas:

1) People are inherently incapable of taking care of themselves.
2) Because Social Security is in place, we don't have to save money—the State will take care of us.
3) People cannot count on their family and friends to help them in case of emergencies. All government programs alienate people in this way.
4) You don't need to invest in yourself—the State will look after your needs.
5) The government is a better steward of *your* money.

Beside the programs that require broken and impoverished spirits for their existence, other aspects of our economic system are also spiritually destructive.

The over availability of credit makes us less productive. I once asked my students the following question which shows just how counterproductive easy credit is: "If you woke up tomorrow and there was no more credit available, what would you do?"

One student replied, "I'd have to save a lot more." Another replied, "I'd have to be very productive very quickly to make money." The implication is that if credit isn't available, people will feel they'd have to be cash rich, save more and become productive right now.

Without our conscious realization, Americans have slowly come to believe that debt is money. If we cannot pay for our bills, we simply take out another line of credit. As long as the Fed keeps rates low and asset prices are artificially high, we have debt to pay for...debt.

"The price of greatness is responsibility." ~Winston Churchill.

Making Things

In the pages above, I've outlined some of the social thinking that negatively affects our ability to make things, to be productive.

Now that we've gotten the counterproductive, negative thought forms out of the way, let's focus on what service or product you can make to transfer money into your bank account. First, there are only three ways for you to be productive:

1) *You can create things with your body (manual labor).*
2) *You can make things with your mind (create ideas, services).*
3) *You can have your money create products or services in your place.*

My purpose in writing you is to show you how to make money with the second and third options, with your mind and your money. Options 2 and 3 only need to be learned once; which is why the current economic collapse is one of the greatest gifts we could've received. Anyone who has owned their own business during the crisis has learned all they need to know to create a life of sustained prosperity.

Learning how money is made is mind work that'll pay dividends for the rest of your life. When you learn to protect and grow your capital, you're protecting and growing your financial freedom. Every dollar you save and invest wisely becomes an employee that you don't have to pay or train. Each dollar hires its own employees and those employees, in turn, hire more.

The initial process of collecting enough of these no maintenance employees is the hardest aspect of becoming financially independent; but the ideas I've shared will help shorten the time it takes to get there by making your current employees much more efficient.

The letters on capital management were focused exclusively on the nuts and bolts of safely compounding the interest you earn on your capital by preserving it. As to what product or service you should make and when to make it has been answered for you in the letters on entrepreneurship. You may want to review them for clues. If you read them to find the right product or service to sell, you'll find it.

"Today knowledge has power. It controls access to opportunity and advancement."
~Peter Drucker.

Making Things: Create Scarcity, Create Demand

I can, however, give you a tip on how to make whatever product or service you choose to sell.

To get the most out of the sale of your products or services, you must be the best at it. Let's face it, competition is an issue with everyone. People want to know how they can create an advantage. We still have only one answer: Create a scarce service or product. Value is scarcity. The scarcer something is the more valuable it is. If you're going to have to sell something, sell something that is scarce.

So the natural question now is, "How do I create scarcity?" The answer to that question was beautifully illustrated by Seth Godin in his book, *The Dip*. His advice is to get through the dip. This is what the dip looks like:

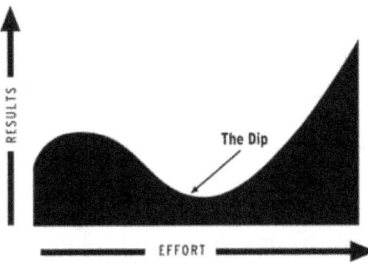

The dip is the in-between stage of initial excitement and completion of a marketable service or product. The dip is when things get hard as you move toward your goal. It's the red tape, regulations, exams, accreditation filings, bankruptcies, zoning, and all other barriers that stand between you and your goal. The dip is the graveyard of most dreams. Without the dip, nothing would be scarce, everything would just be mediocre. And so, as Godin says, it's actually your friend.

The bigger the dip, the fewer the survivors. And the fewer the survivors, the more valuable the service or product you have to offer. If you want to make a lot of money, pick a line of work with a longer, deeper dip few people can get through. If you want to keep the competition out, create a dip that no one else can get through.

"Do your work with your whole heart, and you will succeed—there's so little competition."
~Elbert Hubbard.

The Dip and Investing

Every dollar you earn can go through a big dip or a small one on its path to duplicating itself.

Unlike our labor, our money doesn't have to pass exams, take courses, network, and file permits. It doesn't have to pass through the valley of dead dreams to come out a winner. Here's why: The market makes your money scarce for you. The market can add value to your bottom line without you having to work grueling hours or intense labor.

One of the great benefits of economic literacy is knowing the value of things at any given time. Once you have that intellectual capital, you'll know when to get in and out of markets. You'll know when to buy and hold. When the market goes through upswings and downswings, it's either lengthening or shortening the dip. Swings give you a pass from having to go through the dip or they can make it even longer and harder.

Here's even better news about smart work: The results line stays the same while the effort line contracts. Your money gets to skip a few steps on the effort line.

If you review the letters on entrepreneurship, a good entrepreneur is someone who can predict demand (demand is synonymous with scarcity since when there's a shortage of anything, demand will go up). A good entrepreneur has a way of making the dip smaller (less difficult) by doing something others don't see, by investing when others aren't and by not investing when others are.

"Most people work just hard enough not to get fired and get paid just enough money not to quit." ~George Carlin.

Conclusion

The only question I haven't yet answered is how to distribute your product or service once you've made it—perhaps I'll write on that some day.

In my next letter, we'll discuss the second and more important part of productivity that we've only hinted at in this one.

Your Loving Uncle,
    Akinaw.

Part Five

Making Things: The Secret Ingredient of Wealth Consciousness

The Story Behind
the Money Story

Dear Kidus,

If you were to ask me what the greatest benefit of coming to America was, I'd say it's been learning how to break dance.

No, I'm kidding. Really, the greatest benefit has been the opportunity to expand my consciousness; exploring and learning as much as I can about what I see and what I don't see. When it comes to the principle of productivity, there's the part we do see but there's also a part we don't see.

During my intellectual journey, I came to learn that the things that matter most to us, the things that shape our lives are things we don't see with our physical eyes (nor want to acknowledge with our hearts). We like to pretend that what we see is what we get. We think we live on the first floor of existence but it's all a façade, the real script is being created in the basement. One of the greatest discoveries of the 20th century was the existence of a separate, unconscious world within each of us that animates, controls, and chooses our actions much like a puppeteer does with his strings.

This is how things are made—below the surface. The letter you hold in your hand, your home, your shoes and everything else humankind has made are the remnants of an unseen force that's created things *through* people.

Because what happens in the basement is the real story (the unconscious) and not the party upstairs (our conscious life), any attempt at understanding a given topic (such as wealth creation), must try to find out what's going on downstairs.

If we can find out what's happening below the surface, we will know what things we need to change to create more wealth in our conscious experience. We can work with the unseen forces that make things. We should not leave the deepest parts of who we are on auto drive. We can master it. In all my letters, you'll notice I've been realistically optimistic (despite talking about difficult topics); nothing has changed when looking at the main Actor in economic activity—you. My optimism is based on the psychological finding that our lives are much like movies. All we must do to have the movie end the way we want is to break into the projection room and change the film reels. Once the reels have been changed, the movie (our lives) will also change.

"Success comes to those who become success conscious. Failure comes to those who allow themselves to become failure conscious." ~Napoleon Hill.

What is the *Cause* of Productivity?

So what is the true *cause* of productivity? What makes someone do the things millionaires do? What makes another do the things billionaires do? What makes others do the things thousandaires do?

We only have one answer: "As a man thinketh, so is he." Ideas are not only the lifeblood of the economy, they are also the lifeblood of life. It's the eternal spring from which all human motivation comes from. Every religion and all the success literature of the 20th Century have said one thing: Like a reflection in water, your life is the physical manifestation of your inner state.

Because you cannot have anything that you do not first have *within*, it would perhaps be wise to understand our *soul's* economy.

Success philosophy teaches much more than the fact that internal habits lead to wealth creation. True spiritual teaching also shows us *how* to unlock a seemingly inexhaustible source of inner power.

"A man is literally what he thinks." ~James Allen.

The 64 Million Dollar Question

The big question is this: How are inner, unseen, predispositions formed? How can we be the *type* of person that makes things? How do I make myself the *type* of person that practices the four principles of wealth creation?

If we can answer that question, we can create our internal reality to produce what we want in our external world. Can we voluntarily choose a new mind and a new heart? Absolutely!

We change our inner person by *internalizing* thoughts. Whether we believe prosperous ideas or impoverishing ones, our external world constantly reflects back to us the ideas that are *anchored* in our hearts.

Christian theology teaches the importance of the internalization of spiritual thoughts. It states that, although a person may know God intellectually, that knowledge is not enough to change a person's will. What's needed is a new heart, to be born again in *spirit*, so that what's intellectually known can receive a kind of energy to effect real change. If the inner person hasn't changed, no amount of prodding, counseling, encouragement or other types of external stimuli can change his or her external choices. Being productive, therefore, isn't about external choices or stimuli. The same thing applies to making money—no amount of networking, cold calls, meetings will get you to produce more if somehow, internally you are fighting against the outcome you profess to want.

External reality is merely a canvas, the artist resides inside. The colors you choose, the inspiration for the piece, the brush to be used are all decided on before the external work process even begins.

In this way, you are, as an actor in the economy, working with the world of experience by taking things apart and putting them together to form it into a masterpiece others will find valuable. The world of experience is inert, static and lifeless; it sits waiting for you to do something to it. You can alter it one way or another to suit your purposes. What we see, hear and experience are inconsequential. What matters is your *predisposition* to the world of experience, *to the world of "perceived" facts.*

The promise of wealth consciousness is this: If you can purposefully create a brilliant inner artist, you can create masterpieces at will.

How you *look* at life determines what you do with it, and what you do with it, in turn, determines the level of success you experience. *This is the true cause of productivity. The following story illustrates the 64 Million Dollar Question: If internalized thoughts determine our fates, how does it get internalized in the first place? And how can I use it to achieve success?*

"Self-suggestion makes you the master of yourself." ~W. Clement Stone.

The Power of Internalized Thoughts: A Personal Story

In addition to showing you *how* internalized thoughts "make things", the following story will also explain *why* I made the claim that the economic ideas I've presented to you are the gospel truth. It has nothing to do with my intellectual capacity, any virtue I may have, the hundreds of hours I've put in to understand economics or 13 years of experience in business. You can forget that I'm a college professor or that I have an advanced degree. *None* of this really matters in the end.

There's something else that makes me *absolutely* certain that what I know about economics is the truth. The following is a true story that explains this confidence…

When I was a child, I experienced a traumatic event that's altered the way I look at the world.

In order to appreciate the impact the event has had, we must first do a little background check. Since the time I was born until I was about eight years old, I lived in my mother's shadow. While my sister moved around, living with my grandmother or our older sister, I stayed with my mother. It was virtual paradise for a young child—the exclusive devotion and love of his mother. I loved my mother more than life itself—she was my entire world.

At the age of eight, everything changed in an instant. One day, my father showed up. Although I'd seen him before, I asked my mother who he was, perhaps because it had been so long since he last came around. "That's your father, Akinaw", she said.

My father and his friends sat around and had some coffee. After awhile, my mother pulled me aside to our back porch to talk to me as my father was getting ready to leave.

I could tell something bad was about to happen. My mother kneeled down, looked me in the eyes and said, "Akinaw, you're going to go live in America."

"No, I don't want to go!"

"It's for the best, you must go."

"No, no, I want to stay with you!" I cried.

"Don't worry, you'll be able to come visit me."

Tears welled up in my eyes and I began to cry in protest. I refused to leave. After awhile, my father walked down the hallway, grabbed my right arm and attempted to pry me away from the only person to whom I'd given my heart (up until that moment in my life).

What made the whole event even more traumatic was that I had no warning about what would happen. Almost in a flash, everything I'd loved was taken away.

What happened after that initial event is important to understand: That original experience of loss was greatly magnified in multiple ways.

First, my sister and I had no other relatives when we came to America. In an instant, all our uncles, aunts, fifteen cousins, our grandmother and more disappeared. *Secondly*, most of our life was spent in Simi Valley, CA where there were no Ethiopians at all or other black kids to identify with. *Thirdly*, I had no one to talk to about my experience in order to make sure I interpreted it correctly. I *may* have been asked to talk about the traumatic experience but I didn't want to talk about it because of the pain it brought forward. *Fourthly*, a

172

few years after we arrived, my father and my *new* mom were having relationship difficulties; they separated then divorced.

So, the common theme of my childhood was a painful series of *sudden* and *emotional* losses—my mother, my father, my family, my culture and my new family.

The Effects

That series of losses created psychological effects. As you read, remember that children rarely (if ever), interpret traumatic or emotional experiences positively.

1. Growing up, I kept losing or misplacing just about everything—wallets, money, keys, cameras, jackets, shoes, homework and so on. In class, my mind would wander from one thing to another. Even at home, the inattention and forgetfulness showed up in an inability to complete various chores; a little was done on every project but none was ever finished. This inattention wasn't too difficult to handle in high school but college was a much more demanding academic environment.

    Because the responsibilities of a grown up world were fast approaching, every effort was made to control this inattention.

    Thinking that steel-like determination could fix my outer life, I went to great lengths to force myself to become disciplined. At one point, I even began carrying a ruler around so that when my mind wandered, I'd hit my hand in order to "consequence my mind for inattention." It was a silly attempt at a B.F. Skinner-ish reward and punishment model for behavior modification.

    You may be able to tell why someone with my emotional experience would choose the sanctioning of punishment as a behavioral modifier—it was a lot easier than admitting the painful but true cause of my inattention. Praying, reading the Bible, punishing myself, all couldn't break the inability to focus on any given task.

    The problem became so unbearable, like other people, there was only one thing to turn to in order to enjoy life while avoiding spiritual healing— prescription drugs! After being tested for attention deficit disorder (and passing with flying colors), some relief was finally found (from the symptoms anyway).

    The diagnosis made by highly trained medical doctors was accurate. Multiple tests reinforced the same physical diagnosis. Losing things, inattention and forgetfulness still occurred but much less after the medication. However, there's never a sure way to shut our hearts up. It has a way of continually bringing up *other* events that yell, "Try again! So you don't lose things anymore because you're doped up, but does that hide the fact something is still wrong?" I've learned that we can suppress what's going on in the basement with various types of drugs only for so long.

Our subconscious mind will find a way to let itself out, eventually showing up in different areas of our lives. If we cover one leak in our deceptive scheme to avoid the truth, another, bigger one pops up somewhere else.

2.   As a result of the early, childhood traumatic experience, the doors of my heart closed to the outside world. The great fertile plains of my soul turned into a waterless desert. It was at that young age of eight that that I cried my last, *heartfelt* tears.

For the next seventeen years, my life was at best, zombie-like, uninspired, loveless, unemotional and numb. Even my tears (after that point) were unemotional. The goal in every relationship was to keep people out, to never allow them inside, to never give my heart or my trust to anyone and to avoid all feeling as much as possible.

Keeping everyone out had its costs. On one occasion, after leaving a church group event with some fifty people, I found myself sitting at a red light as empty tears rolled down my cheeks because of loneliness. I had no idea what was going on at the time (I didn't want to know).

3.   Obviously, my dating life was affected by the experience of loss in the sense that it was nonexistent! A lot of confused women have sent me vibes without realizing my antenna was emotionally out of commission.

On one occasion, a few friends were going out and one girl needed a date. As I was sitting alone in my room on my bean bag, playing level 100 of Mario Land on my Gameboy, the phone rings.

"Hey Ak, it's Jesse."

"Hey Jesse, what's up?"

"We're going out and Nicole doesn't have a partner, do you want to hang with us?"

Okay, so Nicole was (without nostalgic exaggeration) one of the prettiest girls in school, something that had not escaped my notice. So what did I do? After looking around for an excuse, none could be found. It was

Friday night, I was alone in my room and because I had been playing Super Mario Land for so many hours, even my bean bag was yelling, "Get off me you fat-ass, you're making me sweat!" In the other corner, my cat (that I had locked in my room to keep me company) was slitting his wrist.

"Sorry Jesse, I'm actually going out with some friends tonight."

4. Even in my religious choices, the experience of loss played a *major* role. In the Protestant camp, there are two major philosophies of God-thought. One is called Arminian (named after the theologian Arminius) and the other is called Calvinism (named after the famous John Calvin).

    I liked Calvinism because it taught that if God wants to save you, it will happen and there's nothing that could keep it from happening. In other words, nothing could pry a believer from God's Kung-Fu grip—there was no conditionality or *possibility* of severance. Calvin even taught that if you've been predestined to be saved, if you're chosen, you *yourself* can't do anything to screw up those plans.

    Because I'd lost the most precious relationship of my life (among other things), it should be obvious why the idea of a personal, eternal and forever relationship with a loving God was so appealing. It stood against the transitory nature of this world of change. I didn't want to believe in a world of flux.

    On one occasion, after reading a small book entitled, *"The Five Points of Calvinism"*, I felt a warm, sweet glow spontaneously fill my heart. It was felt, because after a lifetime of running from the realization of the *impermanence* of love (and the anxiety associated with it), I found something that would *last* (into eternity no less). In my view, on this side of eternity was *Now-Love*, but on the other, *Forever*-Love.

    Lasting Wealth: The emotional need for finding things that last has driven me (unconsciously) to seek out permanent ways of building wealth. It should not come as a surprise that I have a book entitled, *"Of Permanent Value: The Story of Warren Buffett"* on my shelf. The ideas that I've presented in my letters are the surest way of building permanent wealth, something better than I could have consciously come up with.

5. On the opposite side of my office on a book shelf sits a reminder of the "old me." A book on logic full of underlined sentences and notes in the margins. The book was neither assigned for a class nor was it a present. It

was elective reading, bought with my own money when I was twenty years old. Next to it is a book on the history of philosophy entitled, *Thales to Dewey*. Over the last dozen years, I've spent thousands of dollars on books—my appetite for knowledge was enormous.

But why would I do so? What makes a young person give up going to parties to stay home and read about syllogisms, axiomatic systems, Godel's theorem, string theory, and philosophical history? I wasn't making out with girls, drinking beer with my buddies, bowling, cruising or trying out for a sports team. It's not the norm to *choose* to do what I was doing. Here's why I did choose those things…

Because no comfort or joy could be found in human relationships, I turned to books of all kinds. Why books, why knowledge? The most important reason, was because no *one can take knowledge away from you.*

By accident, somewhere along the line, I found out (unconsciously) that knowledge was a thing of *permanent value* and began to "empty my purse into my head." Because knowledge was permanent, *I began to feel again.* At last, I can love something and it couldn't be taken away from me. But I soon found out that no amount of knowledge was ever enough. It was a drug. I was a user. I had to keep learning in order to stay alive. *Life stopped when I put down a book.*

A deep need to fill up the hole drove me to suck into my mind as much knowledge as was possible—history, theology, economics, psychology, epistemology, classics, archaeology, physics, philosophy and much more. *The most intriguing subject for me was epistemology, which seeks to answer how we know what we know and how we'll know we know it when we do. It's an attempt to know what truth is.*

The word epistemology is made up two Greek words—*episteme* (knowledge) and *logos* (study). You can call it *truthology* (this is one of the *most* important things to understand about why the letters you hold in your hands are so valuable).

The reason for digging into knowing *how* we know was to know for sure. After all, in order to *keep* (not lose) what knowledge I gained, it had to be *completely* true. You cannot *keep* knowledge that's been erroneously learned. [In the same way, you can't keep money that's been made based on false assumptions. *I hate false assumptions and would hate for anyone else to have them.* That's part of the reason I've attempted to show you the precise nature of money—you must clearly know what money is in order to preserve it. Economics, what I've tried to teach you in a sneaky way, are the set of assumptions that will determine your financial fate].

Permanent/absolute truth about every topic was my goal (including economics)—it has been the obsession of my existence. It was this goal that led me to stop my MBA program and instead enroll in an M.A. program in theology; it didn't make sense to live my whole life believing something that hadn't been thoroughly examined—especially if it had authority over how I should live.

My focus was never about understanding an entire field of study but finding out if the *ground*, initial *premise* or *foundation* on which the entire thing was based was solid enough for me to invest any time investigating it. If the foundation was solid, all that was built on top of it would also be solid. If it was false, no amount of reshuffling or re-dressing an argument would make it true.

In this way, my mind automatically *economized* or shortened the time it took to know a subject accurately. And I could, therefore, know a field of study or a profession better than those who have labored under false assumptions throughout their careers. Another added benefit was that I didn't mind being wrong—something that most people are deathly afraid of. I *loved* being wrong because it put me closer to the truth. I didn't care about my ego—the more times I was wrong, the sooner I had *lasting* knowledge.

I had a merciless, defiant, fists-clinched, approach to knowing things because knowledge became a substitute for love. When anything was studied, resolute determination was made to find out first whether it could withstand all the logical criticism that could be mustered.

The experience of loss was much more acute in my situation because, even before I experienced any type of loss, I naturally tended to want to keep things to myself. When I last visited Ethiopia, my birth mother said something interesting: "Your sister would share all she had with the other kids until she ran out. But you'd clutch what I gave you and keep it to yourself." This natural 'conservatism' as a child greatly magnified the deep, emotional response to the experience of loss of love.

All of this, however, has been to your benefit, Kidus. What better guide on economic matters than someone with the life experiences I've had. It almost seems like my life was designed for this very purpose.

Now, I don't know if you believe in Providence but there may be something to it. Why else does my name mean "to show the right way, or lead in the right path"? You see, to be able to show the right way, I would have needed to go through a series of *very, very* unlikely events and react the exact way I reacted to every single one:

i. *I was one of very few kids who had the privilege of coming to America.*
ii. *I was naturally conservative as a child, wanting to keep things to myself.*
iii. *Experienced a series of emotional losses (outlined above).*
iv. *Experienced the greatest financial meltdown of my generation.*
v. *The industry that I loved (real estate) experienced the greatest loss of wealth in the recession.*
vi. *I misinterpreted the experiences of loss as a child and created a neurosis.*
vii. *Of all the things I could've substituted for love, I chose knowledge.*

This all has come together either by chance or Providence for your financial benefit. Rest assured that you will notice the truth in my letters when you use it. I've given you all the tools you'll need to protect and grow your capital; it puts you on par with the best economic minds in the world. No one can lie to you or hoodwink you about economics after you've read what I've written because it's a product of a relentless mind. It's not a product of my *own* mind but of a deep pool of wisdom *we can all access* and we do access every minute of every day (I'll explain later). So I can't take *credit* for them, it didn't arise out of my own *conscious* mind. *My story is a clue as to how everyone can access this super mind.*

So you understand a little bit more about how important knowledge was to me, consider this: I did fairly well in school, finished a Master's Degree and a third of an MBA program by my mid-twenties *while struggling with attention deficit disorder.* How come? This question baffled the doctors who were testing me for ADD. They didn't know why my GPA had improved dramatically from high school to college.

They didn't know I fell in love—with knowledge. The answer is that one neurotic symptom (forgetfulness/inattention) was cancelled out by a *stronger* obsession—to have something that couldn't be lost (knowledge). I needed the forgetfulness to deal with the pain of loss while on the other, a blistering, industrious mind was needed to destroy and dismantle arguments until indisputable, permanent truth could be obtained.

This greed for knowledge explains why I can see pages of books in my mind; it explains my ability to recall specific ideas from hundreds of books at will. It explains why the only people to whom I listened were my

178

professors. It was important to listen to them because at any moment, they could blurt out an indisputable fact that couldn't be lost.

6. Carl Jung, the co-founder of psychology once said, "Where love is lacking, power always fills the void." For much of my life, personal empowerment through knowledge was a constant goal. I have a deep passion to empower others because it's a *projection* of my own goal of *self*-empowerment. I actually *care* that people think correctly about things. I genuinely *want* people to be empowered.

"Your life is what your thoughts make it." ~Marcus Aurelius.

Heightened Sense of Awareness

The entire point of detailing my experience here is not to embarrass myself. I've done so in order for you to be confident that what's been said in all the letters up until this point is the gospel truth about money and economics.

My obsession with knowing things accurately has given me the unique ability to give you an accurate report of the true nature of wealth creation in the world of global capitalism. I've paid a terrible price for my *misinterpretation* of the events that transpired early in my life—two decades of virtual nonexistence, a heart closed to love, feeling, and depression. But the consequences that produced the pain have also produced an even greater asset—*a heightened awareness of the mental errors that lead to financial loss (miscalculation).*

This state of mind has given me a unique gift that I can share with the world. After all, we have no limitation but those we recognize. Our greatest difficulty, can be our greatest gift—our greatest struggle, our greatest victory.

It might not be obvious why a heightened awareness of mental errors that lead to loss is an asset. The reason is simple: This awareness of loss brings us back to the principal of entrepreneurship. A good entrepreneur or investor is someone who hedges against risk. We cannot avoid risk if we're unable to identify it.

The greatest investors in the world, as was mentioned, are *oddsmakers*. Of the two billionaire investors mentioned earlier, one (Bill Gross) started his career in a casino and the other (Warren Buffett) was obsessed with math computations, the game of bridge and has been underwriting insurance risk his whole life.

The information you've received from me is, therefore, invaluable because every possible bad money assumption that could lead to a loss of wealth has been explained and *replaced* with good assumptions that will lead to prosperity. Your greatest financial risks have been made clear.

I know it seems that this way of looking at investing or making money seems negative. How can we make money if we continually dwell on negative outcomes? Doesn't that lead to procrastination? Doesn't that lead to fear? No!

We fear the *unknown*, we don't fear what we understand. Understanding all the possible risks doesn't prevent you from making money any more than waiting for traffic to stop prevents us from crossing the street. Remember that the largest payout in Wall Street history was paid to someone who took out insurance against loss!

Profit is really the flip side of having the ability to guard against error. The brilliant real estate developer Donald Trump once said that if you take care of the *downside*, the *upside* takes care of itself. You now know all you possibly need to know to guard against the downside, (losing money) and therefore, guarantee an upside! Remember that when my obsession for knowledge transferred to thinking about business, it didn't stop me from making deals and going for it. On the contrary, it *emboldened* me. *Accurate* knowledge has a way of doing just that.

"We not only interpret the character of events, we may also interpret our interpretations."
~Kenneth Burke

The Trigger That Allowed Me to Serve People

We're all lucky in some way. You're lucky that someone with my background experienced a great recession. It has allowed me to be of service to you and others in ways I never dreamed. Here's how it started.

When the real estate industry came to a complete halt, the fear of loss was triggered in my subconscious mind. As the crisis grew into a catastrophe, all the creative effort and intelligence in the world couldn't help me stay on top. In an instant, the entire industry cratered. Even the older, more experienced real estate entrepreneurs, whom I looked up to, were in deep trouble.

I scrambled to find niche, recession proof income in real estate. After six months of work (giving webinars, blasting the internet with ads) a big deal came my way. It was my biggest, most lucrative deal ever—sixty or so individual deals with an enormous payout. But in the midst of it, the individuals involved in the deal went bankrupt.

At some point during this process, my subconscious mind picked up on something. Without my conscious realization (at the time), it said, "Wait a minute. There's something I don't know. There's a *cause* for everything—there's a *method* to economic recessions and booms. I *must* know it now. I will not waste my life by subjecting my efforts to forces I do not fully grasp."

It realized that the same process I used to deconstruct philosophical and theological ideas or arguments to find the kernel of indisputable truth that *couldn't be taken away*, could be used to understand real estate and economics better than most professionals. The subconscious mind automatically summed up the actual method of building lasting prosperity:

In the real estate business or any business, there is only one thing that we need to know—how to value assets. Knowing the value of assets is like the science of knowing truth in philosophy (epistemology). You've therefore learned the "epistemology of making money." You've learned *Wealthology.*

If you take away any quote from my letters, it's the one by Benjamin Franklin: "I conceive that the great part of the miseries of mankind are brought upon them by false estimates they've made of the value of things."

In the realm of money (and of life in general), our estimates of the "value of things" determines how much we make and how much we lose. My letters have sought to explain what creates or destroys wealth *in order to help you estimate the value of things.* I've found that Squirrelmericans have false estimates of value. That's why ideas of safety and risk had to be redefined. The things that seem to be safe (the dollar, U.S. Treasuries) are really the greatest threats to your wealth.

The ideas contained in these letters are a glimpse of the working of an obsessive mind finding the kernel of indisputable economic truth. You can take it to the bank because it's not a product of conscious thought but of a subconscious one that doesn't make mistakes (*and therefore something I can't take credit for*). You've learned the epistemology of making money. You now know *the* economic truth.

"Our life always expresses the result of our dominant thoughts." ~Soren Kierkegaard.

The Power of the Subconscious Mind

As was mentioned before, everything we see is caused by something we don't see. Behind what's said, is something that's *not* said. *The forces that drive us to do one thing or another happen as a result of internalizing beliefs.* My story was just an illustration of how the subconscious mind works. It is the most powerful tool you have in building wealth (and something most economic textbooks will never cover adequately). The way to influence it to build a prosperous life is to internalize success producing thoughts.

The way to internalize an idea (or turning intellectual truth into heart truth) is through emotion. Our emotionalized beliefs shape our inner person. (In one sense, John Calvin had it right when he said that unbelievers couldn't *voluntarily* change themselves. They first had to be changed internally in order for them to change their choices with respect to divine things).

There's something good and something bad about internalized beliefs. The good news is this: Once beliefs are internalized, they are seared into your subconscious mind as if by an iron. Once that happens, how you react to the external world gets locked into a certain pattern. Your whole perspective—from theology to the movies—becomes *colored by a new lens.* One of the movies that most affected me, for example, was *Eternal Sunshine of the Spotless Mind,* a film about losing the memory of love (as you'd expect given my history).

Our subconscious mind automatically seeks the same things continually, 24 hours a day without stopping, finding delight with the same act as if each additional experience was new. It's because of this fact that reading a logic textbook was a "happy experience" for me.

The repetitive nature of our subconscious activity is a power of its own. Because I was refusing to heal the emotional wound, filling the hole in my heart with knowledge was a constant occupation. As I mentioned, somewhere along the way, the discovery was made that knowledge couldn't be lost or taken away. Once that discovery was made, it started choosing different things for me to do. The subconscious starts where it is with the tools it has to accomplish your goals. I happened to have grown up in the church, so my addiction to knowledge began with learning as much as I could about the Bible.

In high school, I started borrowing books out of the church library. Even then, *a methodical plan for my education was* <u>*automatically*</u> *laid out by my subconscious mind.* It wanted to find out the bottom line, irreducible things that could be known. For example, instead of learning about theology (God-ology), the goal of the subconscious was to know the initial *premise, foundation* or *authority* on which it was built. Were these prophets really inspired? How did we get the text of the Bible we're reading? Are there contradictions? Is religion based on fact or fiction? What about evolution? Quantum physics?

As a senior in high school, I even began teaching myself Greek and Hebrew so that I didn't have to depend on other people's interpretation of the Bible. I began studying archaeology to understand the context in which the original copies of the Bible were written. I went to great lengths to get the story for myself and *I did it all unconsciously* (unaware of my ultimate desire). I did an *insane* amount of work to get the story straight. What was once a chore (reading/studying) was the most enjoyable thing I could do.

What would it be like if creating prosperity could be easy, automatic and a joyful obsession? That's the *promise* of understanding how things are really made, how our *minds* produce things (trust me Kidus, you won't get this in an ordinary economics textbook).

As Napoleon Hill wrote so many decades ago, once our subconscious minds accept certain ideas as truth (through emotional experience), it's an unstoppable force that makes us do things. It will economize time and space to give you prosperity if that is its goal. It will invent things, build bridges, travel continents or anything else to get you from where you are to where you want to be. The great thing is that you don't even have to think about how to get to your destination. I had no idea what was happening to me until years later. The subconscious mind will do it all for you if you can internalize a goal.

Hill says that once this internalization has been accomplished, our minds become "magnetized" to attract everything we need to get what we want out of life. It was only after I became conscious of what I was doing that I was able to understand how this 'magnetization of the mind' works.

Hill's main goal in his book, *Think and Grow Rich*, is to give his readers the tools they need to internalize success principles (thoughts) so that they can magnetize their minds to continuously and automatically create wealth. This is the reason he mentions that making money is *easy* if you can magnetize your mind to automatically attract wealth into your experience. *It has to be an obsession for it to be activated.*

On the flip side, the danger of the way our subconscious mind works is that if we internalize negative thought habits, our mind power gets locked into continuously bringing us what we consciously seek to avoid. We find ourselves doing things we don't want to do as if we were possessed by a will not our own. That other will, or outside force is caused by our subconscious activity.

In my experience, the negative side of internalizing the idea that love doesn't last was the inability to love again. I was afraid of getting into relationships. I was afraid of loving anything too much. The cost of *misinterpreting* multiple emotional experiences has literally been spiritual death.

"Our subconscious minds have no sense of humor, play no jokes and cannot tell the difference between reality and an imagined thought or image. What we continually think about eventually will manifest in our lives." ~Robert Collier.

Your Assignment

Now, we're finally ready to talk about your assignment. If you remember, you were asked to underline and mark ideas that stood out at you regardless of *how* they stood out. In light of all I've said about the subconscious mind, why you were asked to do so can finally be explained.

The exercise is designed to help you find out what ideas are operating in your subconscious without your awareness. What is your subconscious focusing on? What is it bringing into your experience? How are your lenses coloring your experience?

If you can see any patterns in what you've underlined, if any theme stands out in your notes, and especially if you *felt strongly* about any statement I made, you've got a big clue as to how you really view money. If you go page by page through all the letters, you can get a snapshot of not only how the "real you" thinks about money but of the world in general.

This new awareness may provide you with a clue as to what may be holding you back in your pursuit of financial success. On the other hand, the pattern can give you a clue as to what your real strengths are as you pursue prosperity. This awareness may give you a clue as to how you can alter your strategies to be in line with how your subconscious mind is bent.

After looking at the pattern in what you've noted in the letters, sit back and see how that might have showed up in the things you have in your life.

If you give my letters to others to read, please don't mention this exercise. It will not bring others any benefit if their conscious minds know about the exercise in advance. One of the only ways to find out how we really think about anything is to get around the conscious mind which acts like a prison warden. The things it keeps locked up in prison cells are your real beliefs.

Also remember that how we relate to money, shows us how we relate to everything else. It's true that *"money talks."* You may even find your life's purpose as a result of this exercise. Perhaps you've been avoiding something you should look at. Have you been pretending not to know something?

In my case, my experience has shown me that I'm well suited for work as a business and personal consultant. Areas like education, insurance, fund management and especially, investing are natural fits for me. I love solving problems, creating better systems, strategies and I can spot flaws in complicated organizations from a mile away.

I hope this assignment opens your eyes a little bit to how you relate to money and the world of experience.

"How you relate to the issue is the issue." ~Ron Hulnick.

Your Loving Uncle,
    Akinaw.

Why Making Money
Could Be Easy

Dear Kidus,

So far, we've identified *every* possible thing that could affect your financial prosperity—including your subconscious mind, *the principle means of productivity*. The *makers of things* are your deeply held emotionalized thoughts or "Heart Truth".

How to change your thoughts to push you in the direction of your dreams is one of the most important questions to ask and is the last remaining question to be asked in getting a holistic, accurate description of how lasting prosperity is made.

Fortunately, our Creator has given us the ability to control our destinies. It seems the only way to change your inner self is through repeated and emotionalized affirmations of who you want to be and visualization of what you want to create. All other "self-growth" or personal development techniques like forgiveness, grieving, meditation, etc., clear things up so that we are able to accept the truth that will produce the life we want.

After a century of success philosophy, there still isn't anything better than Napoleon Hill's classic book, *Think and Grow Rich,* to show people how to use the power of their mind to get what they want out of life.

The process he advocates is a voluntary or self-administered positive trauma to change the way your subconscious mind works permanently (think about my experience to understand this point). Hill advocates repeating an *emotionalized* affirmation to plant prosperity causing thoughts into our minds. It's just like gardening. When you plant something new, it takes weeks for the new roots to grow into the dirt. In the same way, for an idea to get planted, you'll be required to tediously read an emotionalized statement before the automatic process locks it in (it seems crazy at first but once you do it, your life changes easily).

Once that new idea is locked-in, no more work is required. In fact, you stop working at that point. When I was reading hundreds of books I never *once* felt like it was work. I was trying to figure out how to sleep less so I could learn more. Hill had this theory that I've found to be true from experience long before I had ever heard of him.

187

Now, obviously, many people have succeeded without consciously using Hill's ideas, but that may be because they've accidentally experienced something that wired their subconscious activity to think prosperous thoughts. But for every one person who has become successful by an 'accident of birth', there are three or four that have done it through conscious application of implanting thoughts in their subconscious minds.

In closing my letters, I have but one thing to say—fix your mind on the thing you want, the person you want to be and the things you're willing to do to get what you want out of life.

If you come to the U.S. or if you stay in Ethiopia, you now have more wealth at your disposal than you could ever imagine—*if you recognize it.*

"Dream lofty dreams, and as you dream, so you shall become. Your vision is the promise of what you shall one day be; your ideal is the prophecy of what you shall at last unveil."
~James Allen.

Your Loving Uncle,
    Akinaw.

Postscript

If you want to get more value from the pages you've just read, I have an exercise for you. Take out a piece of paper and write Kidus a letter. You can choose two topics to write about:

a. Imagine that Kidus has just received a visa which will allow him to come and work in America. He also has $100,000 to his name because his father and sister (who live in the U.S.) came into some money and sent him some of their earnings.

   In this scenario, you think he should leave Ethiopia and start a new life here. Using the lessons you've learned about the four principles of wealth creation; write out why he should relocate and what he should do with his money and give reasons for your advice.

b. Kidus is in the same situation but he gets a visa to some other country (you pick); advise him on what he should do with his money. Give your reasons.

As soon as you put pen to paper to complete this exercise, you'll begin to activate a wealth building tool that will soon be recognizable. All you're asked to do is write one letter (at least one page). There's a psychological reason for it.

My goal is for you to get more value from this little book than you'd get from a thousand lifeless, anemic, boring financial or economic books. As you write your letter of financial advice to Kidus, you'll feel something working. To get even more value from this exercise, compare notes with anyone else who might have a copy of this book (even try arguing with them).

Add More Value by Revisiting Squirrelmerica

One of the side effects of my experience of loss has been an obsession to avoid losing time. I've attempted to say more with fewer words. To give readers more value than they'd get from four, five or even ten financial books, I came up with a few creative solutions to economize space. You should know a little about that in order to mine hidden gold from the material.

First, the four methods of wealth creation (capital management, economic literacy, productivity and entrepreneurship) have been created and written in such a way that when one is understood, the other parts become clearer, a lot like a puzzle, a combination or a Rubik's cube. In a way, there are five separate books in one. By combining one major idea from the section on entrepreneurship and one major idea from the section on economic literacy or productivity, you can keep adding value to your financial life. Remember that what you've got in this book is the epistemology or truthology about making money in our economy.

You can participate in letting the book (which is purposefully made to be more like an organism) interact with itself. You're the chemist; as you work with the contents in this book, new (but accurate) ideas will come up.

Second, there are hidden reasons behind every analogy or story that's been included; they are created to teach without out your noticing (to consolidate space). I'll give you a hint by highlighting the most important analogy—the story of Squirrelmerica.

Some of our financial problems result from a misunderstanding of capital. The Squirrelmerica story explains the economy in a much more precise, and understandable way. The Nutconomy only bought and sold one thing (nuts) to better explain how the economy really works. Here's another hint at unlocking the power of the analogy: Compare the Squirrelmerica story with the letter entitled, "The One Thing You Must Understand." By the way, the magician in the beginning of the story is the former Fed Chairmen Alan Squirrelspan, current Fed Chairman Ben Squirrelnanke, the Federal Reserve System and its silent partner the federal government. It's up to you to figure out the rest.

Third, you can use this book as a reference tool to judge the information you get from other financial books and commentators. Most financial commentators and economists are "for profit liars"; their clients are big investment banks. Don't complicate the money making process by listening to their insincere advice.

Fourth, I have stayed away from making technical economic differentiations and terminology. I do know, for example, that there is a *technical* difference between "productivity" and "production". Part of the purpose of this book is to provide a method of creating money in our economic context. I wouldn't want people to go through what I did to get to a place where I can understand the economy.

Lastly, I've personalized economic ideas into more of a motivational book because I wanted to show that what's good for your financial life is good for our nation's economic health. And the story of our collective actions in the larger economy tells us something about the individuals in the society. The reason I've used "the larger economic context" to shed light on our personal finances is because it's a good teaching tool. It's easier to be objective about other people or the State.

I also wanted to make economics easier to get because it's the most important topic to understand for our financial lives. I hope that in five to ten years, if you study money, investing or economics, this material will stay relevant.

Keep Digging: A Note on Wealth Consciousness

Readers who don't have a spiritual/psychological background may not get as much from this book as those that do. So, let me explain the importance of *Wealthology*.

First, I wrote *Wealthology* with the understanding that we can't really learn economics without looking at the main actor in the economy—you. I also wanted to make sure that the benefit you get from this book would last. *Wealthology* is not just about money but also how we *relate* to it. The letter on "Quigley's prophecy", for example, is intended to show how people in every society fail to transcend their economic environment in order to see where it's taking them. We all just get wrapped up in the system even if our actions will destroy the system. That's just how it's been. But maybe, it doesn't have to be that way if enough people realize what we're unconsciously doing to ourselves. The same thing happens in our personal lives.

Wealthology also assumes that there's the you that you pretend to be (conscious life) and then there's the real you (the subconscious). Our conscious minds are just a façade, a projection. It doesn't do anything for us, except rationalize, compensate for what we don't have, for who we are not, protect us from emotional pain and to make countless excuses. The real "power behind the throne" is the subconscious mind.

Wealthology is about empowerment. It seeks to get you in touch with the real you. What you produce in life is not a result of your conscious mind. You are really driven by the subconscious, the *maker of things*. And since "making things" and selling it in the economy is how value (and therefore profit) is created, if you understand the power of the subconscious mind and learn how to work with it, you have a wealth producing asset that'll last.

Almost everyone believes that we have a conscious and a subconscious mind. That's usually where most people stop. But let's keep going.

The reason why I'm so sure that you don't need to read another book on how to create wealth is because the information that is contained in the pages above has been received from the subconscious mind *in a certain way*. The power of repeated emotional experience to get the subconscious to bring a certain thing into your experience cannot be underestimated. So far so good, right? Okay, now, here is where I might lose you.

Our subconscious mind even brings us information we've never learned or experienced. It gives us perfect ideas that we could not consciously produce. *Where does our subconscious mind receive information from?* Why does that "still small voice" always know the right answer? This is where the psychologists, theologians, philosophers and physicists offer their differing opinions because it gets so close to the ground of our being. St. Paul says "in [God] we live and move and have our being." C.S. Lewis made the case that conscience was God's way of getting into the physical universe. Napoleon Hill calls it infinite intelligence. Carl Jung calls it the collective unconscious.

Since I know more about psychology and theology, let me offer my point of view—I have no idea! It's a matter of faith. Whether it's part of God, or whether God has given us a gift or whether it's just a part of Nature or nature, it doesn't matter (as far as using it is concerned). *Either way, working with the subconscious is the only way to create our own destinies.*

Let's just say that we can all tap into a field of something somewhere that we call the subconscious mind which gives us perfect ideas and shows us exactly what we need to do to get what we want.

The way we reach that field of "something, somewhere" is through emotion. Rev. Bernard Beckwith has said that we live in a "feeling universe." I think he was saying what I know to be true from experience—we can access the power of the subconscious mind through emotion. *And whatever emotion we feel the strongest will indicate to us what we'll have the most of in our life.*

Wealthology is a product of my repeated emotional "requests" to have knowledge that I could not lose. It's the thing I have most of in my life.

To show that it doesn't matter *how* you ask for it, as a teenager, I used to pray every night for "knowledge and wisdom"—two things that could not be taken away from me. But I know people who don't believe in God that have received what they wanted through the gateway of the subconscious. They just wrote a statement (as I had done for my prayers) and requested other things repeatedly with emotion and they got it. The things they've received from that "something, somewhere" don't belong to them as surely as *Wealthology* is not a product of my *own* conscious intelligence. At the end of the day what do we really own that hasn't been given to us anyway? Being human is a humbling experience.

I hope this clarifies things a bit. Keep digging into *Wealthology*. Re-read it. It's not an ordinary book that has been consciously contrived. The choice of ideas, words, sentences, phrases, sections, analogies and the people I trust are a lesson *in themselves*. There's a reason for every choice—*even ones I'm not yet conscious of*. I would love for readers to help me get more out of *Wealthology* myself.

Why You Need to Keep Reading this Book

I turned on the news to watch a panel of economists discuss the economy a couple nights ago. As the different people were giving different answers, I found myself feeling like there *might* be something the Obama Administration could do to speed recovery. The important thing I want to bring up is how tempting it is to want the government to "fix things" although their fixes seem to make matters worse. We can't underestimate the unintended evils our government has produced in its attempts to fix things.

The feeling I had was one based on a need to alleviate my fears. If fear can drive us to *want* to believe things that we know are not true, it's all the more reason for us to continually engage in activities that empower us. This book has the goal of putting every reader on par with the best economic minds in the world (at least for the purpose of creating lasting prosperity). Use it. You want to re-read it because fear is the eternal tempter.

Nothing in this book appeals to your fears. Everything in it appeals to the best part of who we really are. If I wanted to write a book that would sell millions of copies without respecting you, I would've omitted the tiny section on foreign policy in these tense times and refrained from talking about the two institutions of welfare and warfare (the sacred cows of two large political parties). I would've said everything was great with the economy or that it was "just a cycle" or "time heals all wounds." I wouldn't have asked you to understand anything substantial or questioned your assumptions. *Remember that there are deep psychological reasons for why I want to tell the truth (it's not just because I'm a good guy) and why I genuinely care deeply that you really understand things as they are.*

You can spend your whole life being intellectually abused and never read what you've read in these pages because the powers that be have an interest in your ignorance.

A Final Note

Nothing I've said should be seen as partisan or political. There's always a great danger in speaking the truth—you'll please no one while angering some people. Please don't radicalize or politicize any statements that I've made.

For instance, someone may take my view that military spending destroys wealth as being anti-defense. It's not. Military spending is a luxury just as a home is a luxury and not an investment. My only goal is to explain the facts, not to take sides. Now on the other hand, I've also said that welfare spending is wasteful and spiritually demoralizing; but I believe strongly in giving. When I was in high school, I volunteered to wake up early to go feed the homeless at a local parish. It was elective. As I got older I also helped build homes in Mexico and supported a child in Africa through the World Vision organization. Today I support organizations like Humanity Unites Brilliance that set up sustainable giving programs (education, micro loans, and clean water) to many parts of Africa. If you think I don't believe in giving, you've got the wrong guy. What I don't believe in is waste.

Government administration of welfare is wasteful because it reduces the amount of money that goes towards human needs and sometimes creates big problems (i.e., Fannie Mae, Freddie Mac and the housing bubble).

Also, please don't think I'm unpatriotic because of anything I've said in the preceding pages. I say this in all sincerity: I'm the most patriotic person I know. *Love and truth are not competing ideals.* Blind zealotry or allegiance has more in common with hatred or control than love.

All these qualifiers have been added because, in addition to the subjects of economics/business, I also teach marketing at the college level. Independent reviewers have more power than ever before. If anyone can read this book and believe I'm politically biased, they must not have read it. If anyone wants to know the economic truth, they have it. A lot of what I've said is disagreeable *to my own prejudices* but I must accept facts for reasons I've already outlined in wealth consciousness.

In closing, thank you for reading this book.

It's a risk to write an honest appraisal of the economic environment in which we live. If you've received any value from the book, please consider telling others about it either in the real world or the virtual one. Independent authors have the advantage *and* disadvantage of honestly serving the people rather than pandering to ideologies, organizations or the ruling elites. We don't belong to one camp or another—we exist for you.

Although it feels good to empower people with accurate, unbiased information, getting publicity is more difficult if you don't belong to one camp or another. We can only succeed in such a politically polarized, extreme world if good, balanced, independent people spread the word. Don't let anyone walk away from this recession without getting something more precious than gold.

Thank You,
Akinaw Bulcha.

P.S., if you'd like to reach me for any reason (speaking engagements, networking, partnerships, business ideas, questions, licensing, suggestions or consulting you can email me directly: akinawb@gmail.com).

If you have any suggestions for the second edition of this book, I want to co-create, enhance it with your comments. If you'd like to find out more about a topic presented in this book, please let me know. Feel free to email me.

You can also visit my blog: www.akinaw.wordpress.com. I named my blog "The Bottom Line" way before I ever thought of writing a book. That fact reinforces everything I've said in the "Wealth Consciousness" section. *Just a hint of why you should "mine" the book for insights that I haven't directly mentioned.* It all points to one definite direction: Getting to the heart of things so we can make it last.

P.P.S., if you don't feel like you've gotten enough value from this book, email me and I'll do my best to make sure you do by filling in any holes.

Acknowledgments

First and foremost, this book would not have been possible without the support, guidance, love and advice of Amy throughout the process. Thanks to my mom for all her love and support throughout the years. Thanks to the rest of my family and friends for support and feedback. Thanks to Greg for reviewing the manuscript. Thank you Joey for giving me ways to make some of the tough parts palatable. Thanks to the Meyers, the Knedliks and others for helping with the title.

Thanks to business and writing consultant Becca Korphage for her insights and guidance.
Thanks to Seth Godin for allowing me to use "the dip" illustration.
Thanks to Nong Vang for helping me format a great cover on a budget.
Thanks to my entrepreneur mastermind group for some great ideas that I've incorporated (Kelley, Michael, Patrick, Julian, Kevin, Don and Edwin).

Thanks to the Mises Institute for making so much great literature, audiobooks, ebooks, videos, and much more available free to inquiring minds. And (*without* endorsing his political ideas) to Congressman Ron Paul for *indirectly* (never personally met him) introducing me (and thousands of others) to Austrian Economics.

Thank You.

www.ingramcontent.com/pod-product-compliance
Lightning Source LLC
Chambersburg PA
CBHW071424170526
45165CB00001B/381